PRAISE FOR
"FROM CHANGING DIAPERS TO CHANGING THE WORLD"

"For more than seven years, Cynthia was a strong voice in my community speaking out in partnership with people living in poverty. Involved constituents like her are invaluable assets to our policymakers. With so many pressing demands in Washington and our state capitals, persistent voices like Cynthia's help drive positive change. Her book can help grow a movement of powerful moms!

I have enjoyed watching Cynthia and the RESULTS Chicago team work their magic. These volunteer activists are always prepared with stories and information needed to make informed decisions about policies impacting the lives of real people. I remember that she even brought her young children to meetings with her until they became advocates themselves! I've come to consider her a friend. Cynthia's methods of activism are the gold standard of citizen engagement and this book is a must-read for anyone looking to get more involved!"

—Congresswoman Jan Schakowsky

"I've always believed that mothers make the best advocates: we're efficient and effective and we're passionate about the safety of our communities. Moms Demand has shown how a movement of mothers and allies working together can influence local and national policies. Levin shares some of those stories and offers clear instructions for impactful actions, so everyone can join in and make the world a better place."

—Shannon Watts
Founder, Moms Demand Action
Author, *Fight Like a Mother: How a Grassroots Movement Took on the Gun Lobby and Why Women Will Change the World*

"*From Changing Diapers to Changing the World* is an important, engaging, empowering book that can help transform concerned moms into powerful advocates. Cynthia Levin breaks down the steps of effective advocacy in an engaging manner, accessible even to people just starting out. Her approach to working with members of Congress will be welcome to moms exhausted or intimidated by political bickering. She tells readers what we at MomsRising have always known: Moms are powerful activists in the fight to improve family economic security, stop discrimination against women and moms, and build a nation where businesses and families can thrive."

—Kristin Rowe-Finkbeiner
Executive Director/CEO & Co-Founder,
MomsRising Together & MomsRising Education Fund
Author, *Keep Marching: How Every Woman Can Take Action And Change Our World*

"As a parent of three daughters, I've said countless times that there should be a rule book for how to do this. The phrase 'WonderMom' is used to cover all manner of excuses why my wife ends up doing everything.

While she might raise an eyebrow if I handed this book to her, I think she'd devour it and give it to her friends."

—**Sean Astin**
Actor, *"Goonies," "Rudy," "Stranger Things,"*
and *"Lord of the Rings"* trilogy
Host, *Vox Populi* political podcast

"This is it. This is the book that awakens moms to our abilities to make our children's world the best we can imagine.

Even before I met her, Cynthia had become a trusted advocate through her ongoing thoughtful communication. Much of my legislation is informed by advocates like Cynthia, real people who provide their stories, concerns, and ideas.

Her book combines warm hugs with laugh-out-loud relatable moments and a clear roadmap for channeling your strength and power. Cynthia will help you navigate the pathway to advocacy so you can join a movement (not bowel-related) and change the world for the better."

—**Missouri Senator Jill Schupp**

"Levin has created a powerful roadmap and inspirational memoir for mom activists and change-agents. She shares how moms can come together to create transformational change in the world, while role modeling and powerfully bonding with their children in the process. I have seen her put these lessons into action as an advocate for the global humanitarian organization CARE and I know, first-hand, that she perfectly embodies the values and the lessons of this terrific book."

—**Michelle Nunn**
President and CEO of CARE USA

"Cynthia uses her personal story and her journey as a mom and advocate to illustrate how one individual can make a real difference in the lives of people around the world, how one mom can affect the lives of millions of moms through perseverance and advocacy. This book is a valuable resource for all of us working for a more just world, and I hope it will inspire people to become the change they want to see in the world."

—Martha Rebour
Executive Director, UN Foundation's Shot@Life Campaign

"A hilarious and inspiring story of how author Cynthia Levin graduated from being an ordinary mom changing diapers into an extraordinary advocate committed to changing the world. A must-read manual for ordinary moms (and dads too) who wish to change this unfair world for the better, but don't know how."

—Kul Chandra Gautam
Board Chair, RESULTS/RESULTS Educational Fund
Former UN Assistant Secretary-General &
Deputy Executive Director of UNICEF
Author, *Lost in Translation* and *Global Citizen from Gulmi*

"There is nothing as powerful as a mother's love for her children. Imagine harnessing that power toward creating a better world for her children. That's exactly what *From Changing Diapers to Changing the World* does."

—Sam Daley-Harris
Founder, RESULTS and Civic Courage
Author, *Reclaiming Our Democracy*

"*From Changing Diapers to Changing the World* is a great resource for everyday people, particularly moms who want to "do something" about the schools in their community, access to affordable healthcare, and more. I'm thankful that Cynthia has joined the ranks of passionate advocates, now teaching and helping others access their government resources.

Having worked for members of Congress on Capitol Hill, I've seen how effective these methods can be in changing minds and policies. This book will guide you and give you the confidence to stay the course during the tough days on the Hill, in your state capitol building, or city hall. I look forward to sharing this book with my network."

—Chonya Johnson
Senior Domestic Policy Analyst, Bread for the World
Lobbyist, Speaker, and Author of *5 Minute Advocate: Access Granted*

"Ever since we met through the UN Foundation's Shot@Life campaign, Cynthia Levin has been a personal guide to lobbying for me. Through her fearless example, I began to call my representatives in New Jersey in support of global and national policies that I cared about and that aided the people who need it most. She showed me that it took just minutes to make a difference. Cynthia's been one of my secret weapons of advocacy, and now this book makes her methods, and experience available to you, too!"

—Jennifer Burden
Founder, World Moms Network

"Cynthia Levin is a powerhouse of advocacy. *From Changing Diapers to Changing the World* is the needed fuel to get mommas to work in creating examples or continuing the legacy of service for their children. There's nothing more energizing than seeing a mom work alongside her children to change the world. God knows, if anyone can do it, WE CAN!"

—LaShaun Martin
National Vice President, Mocha Moms, Inc.

"If we assume that the policy advocacy needed to eliminate poverty, arrest climate change, and accomplish other urgent and worthy goals must be done by experts who can devote their entire lives to this work, we're sunk as a country and as a civilization. Empowering citizens to roll up their sleeves, learn the issues, and speak up for crucial policy changes is our only hope. Fortunately, Cynthia Levin has provided a roadmap for mothers raising kids—and other busy, caring people—to provide the advocacy muscle needed to make the bold changes that are so badly needed. Demystifying activism has never been more important, and Levin gets the job done brilliantly."

—Alex Counts
Founder, Grameen Foundation; Professor of Public Policy,
University of Maryland College Park; and
Independent Consultant to Nonprofit Organizations
Author, *Changing the World Without Losing Your Mind
(Revised Edition)* and *When in Doubt, Ask for More: And 213
Other Life and Career Lessons for Mission Driven Leaders*

"If you think you're too busy juggling as a mom or don't believe you have what it takes to support the issues you care about, just combine your yearning for change with the guidance in Levin's indispensable how-to-advocate book. *From Changing Diapers to Changing the World* is loaded with effective tips, scripts, instructions, and thought-provoking questions, as the author takes you through every step towards becoming a successful "mom-advocate." She also shares personal advocacy stories of dedicated mothers just like you—and herself, who likewise have the desire, but were once unsure of how to make an impact. Apply what Levin reveals in this enjoyable book based on her years of advocacy experience, and you're likely to surprise yourself as you, too, make a difference by addressing elected officials with confidence and ease."

—Pamela M. Covington
Speaker and Storyteller
Life Transition Coach
Advocate, RESULTS Experts on Poverty
Author, *A Day at the Fare: One Woman's Welfare Passage*

"I know the powerful rippling effects of many small actions taken by many ordinary people. I wrote about that in my book, "Give a Little: How Your Small Donations Can Transform Our World." In Cynthia's book, she provides encouragement and guidance to the millions of everyday moms who share a singular drive—to make the world a better place for their children. Mothers are mighty in their numbers and passion, and Cynthia shows exactly how to channel that passion into manageable actions of advocacy. No need to fret over obstacles that seem too large to scale! Many moms together can transform the world!"

—Wendy Smith
Author, *Give a Little: How Your Small Donations Can Transform Our World*
Founder, I've Got You Project

From Changing Diapers to Changing the

WORLD

From Changing Diapers to Changing the WORLD

WHY MOMS MAKE GREAT ADVOCATES AND HOW TO GET STARTED

CYNTHIA CHANGYIT LEVIN

Publish Your Purpose
141 Weston Street, #155
Hartford, CT, 06141

 **Publish** Your Purpose

The opinions expressed by the Author are not necessarily those held by Publish Your Purpose.

Ordering Information: Quantity sales and special discounts are available on quantity purchases by corporations, associations, and others. For details, contact the publisher at orders@publishyourpursepress.com.

Edited by: Gail Marlene Schwartz, Gina Sartirana
Cover design by: Nelly Murariu
Typeset by: Medlar Publishing Solutions Pvt Ltd., India

Printed in the United States of America.
ISBN: 978-1-955985-34-5 (hardcover)
ISBN: 978-1-955985-33-8 (paperback)
ISBN: 978-1-955985-35-2 (ebook)

Library of Congress Control Number: 2021925623

First edition, March 2022.

Publish Your Purpose is a hybrid publisher of non-fiction books. Our authors are thought leaders, experts in their fields, and visionaries paving the way to social change—from food security to anti-racism. We give underrepresented voices power and a stage to share their stories, speak their truth, and impact their communities. Do you have a book idea you would like us to consider publishing? Please visit PublishYourPurpose.com for more information.

DEDICATION

I DEDICATE THIS BOOK to every mother who struggles to raise her children in poverty and to every mother striving to find her own power.

ACKNOWLEDGMENTS

TO DAVID, WHO SUPPORTS my dreams. To Yara and Summer, who enthusiastically join me on this advocacy adventure doing everything I do earlier in their lives and—increasingly—better. To the mom-advocates who both inspire me and keep me laughing: Jennifer DeFranco, Jennifer Burden, Meredith Dodson, Maxine Thomas, Yolanda Gordon, Felisa Hilbert, Pamela Dolan, Teresa Rugg, Laura Frisch, and Sarah Borgstede. To my mother, who took me to League of Women Voters events, ran a public health department during an AIDS epidemic, and showed me that moms absolutely have a role in public policy. To Richard Smiley, who mentored me and gave me supportive encouragement to adapt our methods to include moms and kids. To Willie Dickerson, who never stops believing in me. In honor of the late Bob Dickerson, who believed in me before I believed in myself.

TABLE OF CONTENTS

PART III: ADVOCACY MADE EASY

FOREWORD

Dr. Joanne Carter
Executive Director, RESULTS

Since I first moved to Washington, DC thirty years ago, by far the most important thing I've learned is the power of passionate, committed advocates to affect change. Not paid lobbyists, not PR firms—but thoughtful, informed constituents who move their members of Congress into action.

Any skeptic of that view should meet Cynthia Changyit Levin.

Congressional staff and members of Congress know Cynthia by name and by reputation—for what she does, how she does it, and the impact it's made in the world. And not only is she a brilliant advocate herself but she's also mentored so many others along the way—starting with her own family.

Her motherhood has always been front-and-center in her advocacy. I met Cynthia when she first started volunteering with RESULTS, a grassroots advocacy group focused on poverty, not long after her daughter Summer was born. I've watched her daughters grow into powerful activists themselves, as she brought them year after year to our annual RESULTS International Conference and lobby day to meet their members of Congress in Washington, D.C.

There's a great photo of an old handwritten letter from Cynthia's daughter Yara, when she was seven years old at one of those conferences. She was writing to her senator about a global education bill, and wrote, "Please help kids in poverty go to preschool, because if you don't go to preschool, you won't be good at kindergarten, and if you're not good at kindergarten, you won't be good at first grade. And if you're not good at first grade . . ." Yara continued the logic until she ran out of paper.

That was well over a decade ago now. Yara's gone from writing in marker to now leading congressional meetings and publishing op-eds. And the bill she was pushing for, alongside her sister and her mom and other grassroots advocates, is now law, supporting a better education for millions of children globally.

Shortly after that bill passed through the House of Representatives, a column in the *New York Times* pointed to it as an example of "a story that is virtually absent from today's national narrative: how ordinary people can still influence the government through persuasive moral arguments and tenacity."

The columnist David Bornstein went on to say, "if you're looking to bolster participatory democracy in the United States today, you'd be hard-pressed to find better guidance than the experiences of RESULTS' volunteers." And that kind of guidance is exactly what's at the heart of this book.

How to engage with Congress is not something most of us learned in school. Cynthia has already helped support a new wave of advocates across a whole range of social issues. For thirteen years, I've watched Cynthia learn skills and strategies—from mentors and through sheer persistence and dedication—then teach them to others. And when she sees successful new tactics created by high school students in her city, she shares their success with our national trainers, so advocates all over the country can benefit.

When she moved to St. Louis, there were no RESULTS advocates working on global poverty issues in the area. Today, the St. Louis group is a media powerhouse, leading the way nationally because of Cynthia's coaching. They're moving members of Congress from both parties across Missouri into action (and they're doing the same across the border in Illinois and beyond, for that matter).

In RESULTS work, I've seen that the more thoughtful and personal the action, the more power it has on Capitol Hill. Cynthia embodies this in her approach. And now she's taken the best parts of all she's learned and put them together for the audience that I know is dearest to her heart: moms.

I've had the great privilege to call Cynthia a friend and learn from her work over many years. And I'm confident that through this book, so many more people will be able to do the same—learning not just the mechanics of advocacy, but the skill and art of it, from a mom and an advocate extraordinaire.

INTRODUCTION

WOULD YOU LIKE TO join a movement of powerful moms who are changing the world, one conversation at a time? While society is struggling with a lack of empathy, equity, and justice, mothers are rising up to be voices of reason and compassion. Together, we can:

- Create a better world for our kids
- Engage our families in activities that cultivate generous hearts
- Have meaningful dialogues about something other than diapers, daycare, and dinner plans
- Uplift other mothers while empowering ourselves

My sisters in motherhood, I'm glad you are here. We have incredible power to shape our own destinies and influence the future of our world. We can be more than consumers and stereotypes. We can shape opinions in our communities and inspire actions for global transformation. We can be *mom-advocates*. For all you moms who want to get started making the world a better place, let me introduce you to a special kind of volunteering called *advocacy*.

You may not be familiar with that word, but at its core, advocacy is simply expressing yourself to inspire action from another person with the power to help. It involves showing up when it counts and saying what you believe. Whether you prefer to express your opinions by handwriting a thoughtful letter, making a quick phone call, sitting down face-to-face with your senator, or organizing a playdate phone bank, you can use your mom skills and experiences to influence our national conversation and define the future our children will share.

Regardless of educational background, employment status, outward appearance, or inner beliefs, mothers of young children want to give kids secure lives full of opportunities. When moms get together and combine this mutual motivation with individual passions, we can bring about the change we envision.

Although there are many dad-advocates I respect and admire, I'm writing this book for mothers for two reasons. First, motherhood is my own personal experience and the one I know best. Second, I want to promote a new path for moms who have trouble seeing their own potential to influence.

I encounter a distressingly high number of mothers who wrestle with power and self-identity issues as they navigate shifting expectations in professional and domestic roles. While this can be frustrating, motherhood also enables women to redefine our roles in life and create new visions of ourselves. Becoming a mom-advocate can introduce us to new skills, new ideas, and new purpose during this time of natural transition.

When I first became a mother, I was a highly educated woman married to a loving husband, assured of a stable income, and living in a safe neighborhood. Despite my security, motherhood shook my self-assurance and stripped me emotionally bare anyway.

At no time in my life before or since have I ever felt less confident, less capable, and less sure of the future.

During those long, sleepless nights, I began to realize that somewhere a mother was feeling exactly what I was feeling, except, unlike me, her fears were her reality. Clean water, food, heat, doctors, medicine, a safe place to sleep free of war and violence—I had all of these things and still felt vulnerable. How was it fair for me to worry when others lacked so many basic resources I took for granted?

Over the course of my daughter's infancy, I resolved to do *something* to support mothers who loved their children as much as I loved my tiny girl but had far fewer resources to offer them.

My journey started with baby steps: making small monetary donations and writing a few letters. Gradually, I moved from hopelessness and vulnerability to action and empowerment, from clinging to my baby in my bedroom to striding around Washington, D.C. in a powerful partnership with mothers living around the planet.

After nine years and a lot of trial-and-error lessons in activism, the United Nations Foundation invited me on a trip to meet moms and babies in rural Uganda. Seeing the love those women had for their healthy infants assured me that I had actually managed to turn my own fears into positive action for a generation of new mothers.

My goal today is to inspire American moms to think of themselves as mothers to our communities and our nation. I'm writing this book to help other women become the change they want to see in the world. I spent too many years aimlessly wondering what to do and how to do it. I want to help you skip right past those questions and frustrations. I'm sharing my story and the lessons I've learned along the way to clear the path for you and make your journey easier and a bit more comfortable.

Most mothers, especially those with young children, crave both convenience and empowerment. Advocacy can be both convenient and empowering, especially if you utilize the advice that follows!

How To Use This Book

These pages hold the insights learned during my transformation from stay-at-home mom with a baby on my hip to global activist with my teen-advocates by my side. Whatever issue you choose to address—hunger, climate change, systemic racism, paid family leave, or so many others—this book will equip you to become an agent of change *and* a great role model for your children. You won't follow the exact same path I did because we all have different lives, personalities, and challenges. My intention is not to provide a one-size-fits-all model but to provide you with inspirational stories and tools to help you find your own way.

I work mostly on global causes, so much of my advice focuses on interacting with U.S. senators and representatives to influence national and international policies. However, many of the actions I describe work just as well at the state, county, city, school board, and neighborhood levels. Learn the basics from this book and then boldly and creatively adapt these general principles to fit your own situation and personality.

The book is divided into three sections. Part I explains why mothers make great advocates. Part II helps you figure out how to get started. Part III provides practical advice for taking some basic yet powerful steps to change your local or global community. This "Advocacy Made Easy" section serves as a quick resource guide.

I didn't become the advocate I am today by myself. Not only did I have great coaches, but I also met extraordinary mothers along the way who inspired and influenced me. Learning from them allowed me to adapt my own strategies and understand how other people use different tactics to achieve the same ends. Their day-to-day lives may not look like mine, but we all share a passion for shaping our society into something better to share with our kids. Throughout the book, you will find profiles of some of the mothers I most admire so that you too can learn from these remarkable women. You'll also encounter "Storytime" sidebars with real-life stories offering glimpses of moms advocating in the midst of everyday life.

I hope that this book inspires you to 1) take action and 2) bring other moms with you into advocacy, encouraging each other to take small steps and build large movements

With hope #1 in mind, I hereby give you permission and even encouragement *not* to read this book in order. If at any point you feel moved to act, flip to the third section, choose an action, and do it. You don't have to wait until you've read the book cover to cover. If you feel motivated and can't wait to get started, then by all means jump in before you talk yourself out of it!

As for hope #2, I have included questions for discussion throughout the book to prompt further reflection. Of course, you can read this book alone, but there is great strength in sharing ideas with other women. Gathering a group to read and discuss this book is a great way to start building your own community of advocates. Look to faith organizations, moms' groups, neighborhood book clubs, and local chapters of advocacy associations to find thoughtful people who might be interested in exploring these ideas about mom power. Create a space where you can discover your personal influence and grow the movement of mom-activists.

If you truly want to create a better future for you and your children, I challenge you to become the hero reflected in the eyes of your child. Let go of those hopeless feelings, put on your Supermom cape, and start saving the world with me.

PART I

WHY MOMS MAKE
GREAT ADVOCATES

"THIS'LL BE QUICK," I ASSURED myself as I juggled my baby and a diaper bag full of letters to my congresswoman. My daughter wasn't yet walking, so she rode along gamely on my hip as we shoved open the door to U.S. Representative Jan Schakowsky's office in Evanston, Illinois.

As my church's new Bread for the World organizer, I was carrying a hundred or so letters urging our congresswoman to use the power of the U.S. government to fight hunger. I had learned that delivering handwritten letters in person makes more of an impression than simply dropping them in the mail, so I packed up my baby and our letters and made the trek to Evanston. Little did I know what kind of impression I was about to make.

The office lobby was bare save for a few flags, a lot of pamphlets, and one very visible telephone that visitors were obviously expected to use to announce their arrival to aides on the other side of a security door. "Hang on, honey," I soothed my increasingly squirmy girl as I perused the options on the phone. I found the correct number and dialed the extension, then took a seat to wait. I settled the baby in my lap and started to mentally rehearse my little speech about poverty until a loud flatulent trumpeting and a horrible smell announced the source of my daughter's discomfort.

With horror, I realized that she'd filled her diaper to a truly spectacular level. Before I could move, I saw the doorknob to the office ominously beginning to turn. There would be no time to remedy this smelly situation before the staffer walked through the door into the small room that was quickly filling with an overpowering odor.

A professional-looking aide entered the room with a wide smile and greeted me formally. I can't tell you exactly what I said next, but I know I made some sort of mortified apology for the incredible stench emanating from the adorable child now happily crawling on the floor. It's incredible to think that this embarrassing episode would turn out to be one of my most fortunate moments as a volunteer lobbyist.

I soon learned that the aide had a daughter just a bit older than my own. He immediately recognized the cause of my distress and began laughing in a with-me not at-me kind of way. The aromatic episode certainly made our meeting stand out amidst all the other routine parts of his day! We forged a bond as parents that set the tone for how we would work together on child survival and education issues for years to come. Who knew that an outburst of poop could initiate a relationship that would help bring food, medicine, and education to millions of children in poverty? I had never anticipated that mommy mishaps could lay the groundwork for influencing international policy.

When you are in the thick of caring for infants, everything seems to come back to diapers. You can leave the house looking your shiny best, but sooner or later—and sometimes at the worst moment—you will find yourself changing a dirty diaper. Please don't misunderstand. I'm grateful that my children enjoyed healthy infant years with the blessing of vigorous digestive tracts. I also appreciate that changing diapers can be—in its own way—a noble

Meeting with Dave Davis, Congresswoman Schakowsky's constituent advocate, in the same room where we first met over a dirty diaper.

and sacred activity. But I'm not sure I've ever run into a mom who gleefully announced, "Time to change my baby's diaper! Definitely my favorite part of raising an intelligent and caring human being!"

Whether your diapers are cloth or disposable, it's still the same thing over and over again with a cyclical redundancy that feels never-ending and menial. How can you contribute to society when so much of your day is consumed by diapers? During my babies' early days, I often felt there must be something more meaningful I could be doing in addition to filling the micro-waste management position that I had created with my husband.

I'm happy to report that I eventually discovered plenty of advocacy actions I could be doing while in that challenging stage of life. And as my children grew out of Pampers and into big-kid underwear, I was able to gradually grow out of the role of diaper changer and into the role of a world changer. It was just hard to catch a vision of this life in those early months of motherhood.

In those days, I'm not sure I even knew what the word "advocacy" meant. Before we dive into the depths, let me give you my quick definition: **Advocacy is expressing yourself to inspire action from another person with the power to help.**

Of course, you can lift up a wide range of needs to inspire actions from a wide range of people. I chose to advocate to elected officials for two reasons.

First, I can have a much bigger impact as an advocate in government than I can as an individual. When my voice helps influence policy, I play a part in changing systems to help thousands or millions of people in need. If I can convince federal decision-makers to support funding for effective programs, I'm directing more money than I would be able to donate in a lifetime.

Second, legislative advocacy plays a huge part in my own personal empowerment. Early motherhood was a time of immense change for me, and not all of it was good for my self-esteem. It was a time of intense soul-searching, self-doubt, and uncertainty accompanied by a painful awakening to the widespread issue of poverty. When I connected with a strong network of mentors who taught me to engage powerfully with elected officials, I felt more confident than ever before!

I want this transformative experience to be available to every mom, especially those of you who might be feeling insecure or bewildered at the life changes motherhood brings. You might be surprised that you have already been developing the most valuable tools you need for this work: the persistence you cultivated while dealing with newborns and the patience you nurtured while negotiating with toddlers. The love and frustration you experienced in those repetitive battles fostered incredible power that you can tap into when dealing with Congress.

Notes

CHAPTER 1

HOW I BECAME THE "ANTI-POVERTY MOM"

THERE'S A WORDLESS LULLABY I used to listen to while feeding my firstborn. I discovered "Hace Tuto Guagua" on an album of world music for mothers, which included pieces in English and in languages I had never heard.

The song is just a simple melody in a round beginning with one voice that sounds like a woman humming intimately to a baby. More comforting voices soon join in, wrapping the original voice in a loving blanket of support. Harmony is added as more women, men, and instruments combine to create a rich tapestry of sound until the song peels back to the first voice—alone and sweet.

In the deepest hours of a cold Chicago winter, I listened to this lullaby as I sat alone in the dark, breastfeeding my newborn daughter and wrestling with irrational fears. Postpartum hormonal changes and sleep deprivation compounded my worries about whether she would continue breathing through the night and whether I could ever be a good mother. Although there were no logical reasons for me to doubt myself, I wondered if I could keep my daughter alive for even a year.

The wordless song comforted me and helped me realize that so many mothers have these same worries—and that we don't have to bear them alone. The beautiful melody made me feel connected with mothers across distances and throughout time. Listening to it, along with songs from all around the globe, opened my mind to consider families in other countries and cultures. It occurred to me that while the fears were universal, the resources we have to care for babies are not. In those moments when I felt like I might shatter from anxiety, I got my first glimpses of the heartbreak felt by mothers in such extreme poverty that they cannot meet the basic needs of their children. What good would it do for me to dwell on irrational fears when another mother faced actual danger? Could I become part of the loving chorus taking care of her and offering hope? Answering these questions set a new course for the rest of my life.

Every mother will tell you that having a baby changed her life in some way. Of course, I expected it to change me; I just never anticipated that motherhood would cause such an upheaval to my career, my worldview, and my confidence in myself. Or that the upheaval would wind up all for the better!

In December 2003, my husband and I took a gamble, leaving our jobs and starting his new business at the same moment we were having our first baby. I had been a mid-level engineering project manager for an automotive supplier in the suburbs of Chicago. Considering that co-workers were being laid off from my company with alarming frequency, it wasn't a tough decision for me to close that chapter of my life.

Yet leaving the workplace to care full-time for a newborn during a Chicago winter left me both physically and emotionally isolated. Most days I felt too tired and fragile to even leave the house. National Public Radio became my lifeline to the outside world because of the wide range of information and humor I could get without changing the station. After all, where else can you get free access to insightful political commentary and a science-based story about a hypothetical robot battle between Mars rovers?

Tuning in to NPR while home with my newborn gave me a way to learn about pressing global problems that I never made time for in my working life. Unrest in poverty-stricken Haiti and a refugee crisis in Sudan were frequently in the news during my baby's first year, and I had a hard time hearing about these situations without breaking down in tears. These strong emotions were telling me that I should do something, but I felt utterly powerless.

Days after we blew out the candles on my daughter's first birthday cake, the massive Sumatra-Andaman earthquake and tsunami in the Indian Ocean killed more than 200,000 people and impoverished millions of others in countries already struggling with extreme hunger and disease. I was starting to understand that mothers who lived in extreme poverty or in conflict-torn areas all too frequently never survive to see their baby's first smile.

For a few years, I faithfully donated modest amounts of money to various poverty-fighting organizations, but we weren't wealthy people, and writing a check never seemed like doing enough. Was there more I could do? How could an ordinary person like me possibly help with such big problems?

My questions set me on a path to help millions of moms in need.

Primed to Care about Poverty

Even before I became a mother in 2003, I had cared about hunger and poverty. I volunteered in ways that fit conveniently into my social life. Before my daughter was born, I served meals at my church's soup kitchen. I sat on a committee that organized lively, swanky fundraisers for the Greater Chicago Food Pantry, allowing us to raise money while also giving us a chance to wear little black dresses and cute heels.

Still, in my bubble of privilege, I had not been ready to empathize with parents in poverty nor to seek out real solutions to poverty and act on them. But my daughter's birth left me caring for a new baby while disconnected from the pressures of my old professional life and out of step with the rhythms of my working friends. I became open to deeper feelings.

The combination of seemingly endless moments of solitude and the newfound maternal love that had exploded in my heart gave me space to make new mental connections and draw startling conclusions about the world outside my own security. Somewhere, I heard that more than half of the world lived on less than two dollars a day. I began to internalize what that meant for families living inside that cold statistic. It was both energizing to open my eyes to the problems of the world and heartbreaking to not know what to do about them.

In random interludes between feeding my baby and cleaning the house, I searched online to learn what I could about global poverty. Data I would previously have skimmed over grabbed my attention. Instead of glossing over a statement that one-third of the world's children under five suffered from stunted growth due to hunger, I'd reach out to thoughtfully rub my baby's head.[1] My finger would caress the fontanel, the squishy spot on the top of her skull, as I remembered my panicked call to the doctor when it had sunk in from lack of milk during her first week of life before we had the hang of breastfeeding. I'm embarrassed to admit this was the first time I had reflected deeply about the emotion any mother would feel when watching her child suffer from hunger.

Shame on all of us, I thought, for letting this happen. Shame on me for not knowing earlier and for not saying anything about it after I knew more. Feeling that burden, I started talking about these realities to friends and my husband. But still, I didn't *do* anything. What *could* I do?

Another Daughter, More Resolve

Almost two years later, I welcomed a second daughter into our world. By then, my attention was easily captured by any poverty-related news stories with strong emotional connections. I still recall cradling my baby in a rocking chair while listening to a story about a twenty-one-year-old widow in Kenya responsible for thirteen children from her extended family.[2] All of their parents had died of malaria or other diseases. That year also brought the devastating Kashmir earthquake to Pakistan, which killed an estimated 80,000 people.

---

[1] World Health Organization report, "World Health Statistics 2020: Monitoring Health for the Sustainable Development Goals."

[2] "Chicago's Promise to Kenya," WBEZ 91.5 Chicago, February 13, 2007.

I was hearing these types of stories with receptors to truly listen. Plus, the sleepless nights, breastfeeding challenges, and trying situations of motherhood were toughening my resolve to do something. A perceptive friend from my church noticed my growing interest and invited me to join Bread for the World, a Christian advocacy group that organizes congregations to write letters urging members of Congress to fight hunger around the world and in the United States.

Bread for the World had ideas for poverty solutions and Congress had the power to make them happen. Here were Bread volunteers at my church telling me that I had the power to make Congress act. This was exactly what I needed to hear.

The organization's website showed me easy ways to get involved on my own time without having to go to any meetings or pay for a babysitter. Sample letters allowed me to dash off hand-written letters to senators when I couldn't go back to sleep after a middle-of-the-night feeding or diaper change. I could use a telephone script and make a two-minute phone call to Congress while my babies napped. I was so relieved to find there was something I could do and delighted to find it didn't take much effort!

After a few months, I got up the nerve to follow Bread for the World's instructions for writing letters to the editor. These are short notes submitted to a newspaper by a reader stating an opinion about an issue. Such letters can help get the attention of local leaders and politicians, and I wanted to publicly encourage my congresswoman to help hungry people.

Formerly a technical writer, I was comfortable reporting facts but not used to writing anything unless I was a subject matter expert. It was a daunting task to write a 150-word opinion piece, and I had a hard time imagining why a newspaper would print the words of an unemployed housewife, which is how I viewed myself back then. I must have fiddled with my letter for hours before I got up the courage to push send.

To my utter shock, it was published that week in my tiny local paper! That validation felt fantastic. Maybe I had something to say after all. Timidly, I submitted another letter the next month to the same newspaper and saw my name in print a second time.

Swelling with confidence from my early success, I started responding to any newspaper article I could find that was remotely related to poverty. My next forty-two letters went unpublished, but the forty-third was printed in *The New York Times* right under one written by Speaker of the House Nancy Pelosi! My headline read, "Children in Poverty: There Is No Excuse." It was an enormous boost to my self-confidence. If those prestigious editors believed my words had merit, then I figured I should believe in myself as well.

My children quickly discovered I didn't mind quiet cuddles while I wrote letters to the editor on my laptop.

Bursting with pride as I looked at my name in *The New York Times*, I would have opened up a bottle of champagne if I had any. Sure, writing for newspapers was harder than making phone calls, but I could write from my computer at home in my pajamas and actually contribute to the national conversation about poverty.

Advocating in Person

The heady feeling of validation from seeing my name in print prepared me to feel worthy to take the next big step: the 2007 Bread for the World Gathering in Washington, D.C. Nancy Hagstrom, the Bread for the World organizer at my church, asked me to attend on behalf of our church to learn more about poverty and visit members of Congress. It sounded both intriguing and terrifying. Writing was one thing, but talking to a senator in the same room? Yikes. Besides, I had obligations to my family. Nancy listened patiently to my protests that I could not afford the trip and could not leave my young kids on weekdays when my husband had to work.

Then, one day she unexpectedly turned up at my doorstep with a personal check for $100 and information about applying for a partial scholarship to help me cover the rest of my travel expenses. What could I say to that? It is incredibly powerful when someone reaches out to say, "I have faith in you. I have solutions. I believe you can do something extraordinary!"

I recognized this as a turning point. I could continue to lament the state of the world and passively wonder what more I could do, or I could take a leap to a next level. This woman I hardly knew was taking a chance to remove barriers to my growth. Could I have enough faith in myself to take up her challenge? Didn't I love the church song, "Here I am . . . I will go, Lord, if you lead me?" Could I have faith in God calling my bluff and calling me to action? Yes. I could keep that faith.

I really didn't want to let Nancy—or God or myself—down after her big gesture, but in reality, $100 doesn't go far when traveling to D.C. I applied and received the scholarship to cover the conference registration. I also appealed to my church, which supplied my plane ticket using airline points on the church's credit card. Before I knew it, I was on a plane clutching a special Africa-themed issue of Vanity Fair with Don Cheadle on the cover, guest-edited by Bono, containing everything a beginning activist needed to know about global HIV/AIDS and poverty.

The trip changed my life. Meeting hundreds of other people who cared so much about hunger and disease was incredible. I partnered with activists who were in touch with their faith and were also morally outraged at the injustice of poverty. Their enthusiasm was both comforting and inspiring.

Like me, most of the participants were backed by churches full of supportive congregations. Feelings of isolation melted away as I realized my actions could join with thousands of others to create a genuine force for social change. Lack of childcare meant I had to return to my kids before the organization's scheduled visits with members of Congress, but I decided to return the next year and stay long enough to participate in those meetings.

I was disappointed when Bread for the World did not organize a D.C. gathering the following year. Fortunately, my Bread connections from the first year told me an organization called RESULTS could teach me how to successfully meet with members of Congress face-to-face. RESULTS specializes in encouraging volunteers to develop personal relationships with their senators and representatives, which hardly seemed possible to me at the time. I also discovered that RESULTS addressed a whole host of global issues beyond hunger, including HIV/AIDS and education.

When I took the leap to attend the RESULTS International Conference in D.C., I was blown away by the passionate and intelligent people I met. Most were from ordinary backgrounds, but all had the audacity to expect members of Congress not only to meet with them but also continue to work with them throughout the year.

I could not believe the boldness RESULTS volunteers displayed while urging Congress to increase nutrition, medicine, and healthcare for impoverished mothers. It was so daring and far-reaching. Three days of training prepared me to speak powerfully on issues I had been thinking about for years. Chicago advocates Richard Smiley and Oscar Lanzi guided me through an entire day on Capitol Hill with five meetings, including my first exhilarating face-to-face sit-down with my own U.S. Representative, Congresswoman Jan Schakowsky. *This* was what I wanted to do!

Learning from Difficulties

Of course, it was not all smooth sailing. In real life, going out on a limb to try something new almost always includes some down days along with the thrilling ones.

My lowest day might have been on October 17, 2009, when no one—not a single person—showed up for the event I organized to support a global anti-poverty campaign. I sat alone in the office space I had reserved, eyeing my spread of homemade guacamole and brownies, listening alone to a webcast featuring the inspiring Dr. Paul Farmer. When an organizer ended the broadcast by encouraging listeners to physically rise and commit to "Stand Up, Take Action, End Poverty Now," I remained prone on the office couch, feeling like advocacy's biggest dope.

Luckily, I had supportive coaches who picked me up, put me back together, and taught me how to improve my outreach. They taught me that these low points would eventually make me a much better activist and coach. I have the empathy and the street cred now so that people believe me when I say, "Keep going. Try different things. It gets better."

I am grateful that I had a tremendous support system of peers and coaches at RESULTS to buoy my spirits and encourage me to stay involved when my own self-doubt was telling me to quit. Finding encouragement, staying inspired, and being persistent are the keys to making progress.

The idea of support was so important to Sam Daley-Harris, the founder of RESULTS, that he incorporated it into the name of his organization. RESULTS was originally an acronym for "Responsibility for Ending Starvation Utilizing Legislation, Trimtabbing, and Support."[3] The organization has abandoned that longer title because today it focuses on much more than starvation and because no one ever uses the nautical term "trim tab" in conversation. Nonetheless, "support" remains a core value of the organization. Sam knew volunteers needed support to stay engaged long enough to become truly empowered and make a great impact on ending poverty.

When Lisa Marchal, a RESULTS Grassroots Impact Manager, and I presented an "Advocacy 101" session on a college campus in downtown Chicago, a young man in the front row raised his hand to confess, "One time I held a meeting and I was the only

---

[3] A "trim tab" is a nautical term referring to a small rudder that makes adjustments to assist a bigger rudder in the steering of a large ship. Here, "trimtabbing" is a metaphor for engaged citizens influencing members of Congress to assist in the steering of the government, sometimes referred to as the "ship of state."

one who came." I looked at him with compassion and said, "Yeah. Me, too." Then I smiled at Lisa, who had consoled me after my zero-turnout meeting. My missteps help me relate to others so I can convince them to keep going.

In my dark days, it took some encouragement from my mentors and friends to continue. But I did, and I learned to be creative so I could meet the needs of other moms while also recruiting them to my cause.

I started monthly playdate/letter-writing sessions called "Social Justice for Social Moms." While a babysitter watched our kids, we discussed a justice issue and wrote to elected officials. These sessions with neighborhood moms gave me hope that I wasn't the only one who cared about more than potty training and preschools, and they gave us a chance to take action while still honoring nap times.

To engage friends who couldn't make it to our playdates, I began writing "The Anti-Poverty Mom Blog." The title wasn't so catchy, but it was a great place to share my published letters to the editor. I could also share videos about issues and advocacy actions from organizations I liked. It was my first step in building a reputation as a mom-advocate.

Traveling to Africa with Shot@Life

Over time, I began to take small leadership steps and meet more influencers by attending events and engaging in social media. My networking took a leap when I was invited along with thirty-five other moms to join the first class of "champions" trained by the United Nations Foundation for a new global immunization campaign called Shot@Life.

Motherhood was the uniting factor in our selection to help launch the nationwide Shot@Life campaign promoting vaccines to protect kids in poverty worldwide from four killer diseases: polio, measles, rotavirus, and pneumococcal virus. I loved that the campaign was tailored to encourage and celebrate moms, and I happily asked my members of Congress to provide funding for global immunizations.

My six years of activism reached new heights when Shot@Life invited me and seven other moms to witness UNICEF family health programs in Uganda. Our mission was to talk with Ugandan mothers so we could share their stories back home. Frankly, I was apprehensive as I tend to shy away from international travel to countries where I don't understand the native language. I was—and still am—one of the least well-traveled global activists you'll ever find. But even more than being afraid, I felt honored. This was my big chance to share words with a few of the "faceless" mothers I had helped but never expected to actually meet.

Of course, they did have faces that reflected the same love and concern I felt for my own children. The resilient women we met expressed gratitude for the lifesaving vaccines and HIV/AIDS medications provided by Americans. Thanks to aid supplied by a minuscule percentage of U.S. taxes (less than 1 percent of our national budget is used for poverty-focused foreign assistance), these mothers no longer lose children to measles and polio; that nightmare scenario I'd played out in my mind so many times in the comfort of my bedroom.

In fact, they had shifted to thinking about education instead of wondering if their babies would live to be six. They were grateful for vaccines, and their next strongest desire was to find a way to keep their children in school so that they could enjoy brighter futures as adults.

It startled me to realize I was the target of their lobbying! They were using the opportunity to convince me—an American citizen with influence over my government—to help educate their kids. Their testimonies cemented my belief that advocating not only allows babies to survive, but also helps families to thrive. Their resolve crystallized my focus.

These personal stories from Uganda echoed some great news rarely reported in American media: extreme poverty was in decline, and the survival rates of mothers and children were rising at the beginning of the 21st century. The number of women dying in childbirth decreased by half since 1990, thanks to a worldwide push for resources, including more trained healthcare workers assisting

Getting to know a family of children at a mosque in Fort Portal, Uganda, as they wait for medical services.
Photo credit: Stephanie Geddes.

during births, better prenatal care, improved maternal nutrition, and increased access to birthing kits. The number of children dying before age five was reduced by more than half between 1990 and 2020 due to interventions such as vaccines, access to clean water, and better nutrition in a baby's first 1,000 days.[4]

But make no mistake—progress like this happened only because of the persistent activism of everyday people like you and me. Never fool yourself into believing that our government (or any other government) would have done all of this *anyway*. In 2020, political will for U.S. foreign assistance wavered when COVID-19 put Americans' lives at risk. At the same time, the pandemic disrupted life-saving health interventions worldwide and threatened to undo hard-won gains in maternal and child health. Sure, a handful of senators, representatives, and even some presidents keep an eye on extreme poverty issues. As a whole body of elected officials, however, they do not naturally unite to help the most vulnerable people. I've learned that it's *our* job to pressure our elected officials in solidarity with the people who need it the most.

Raising Advocates

My daughters learned along with me that easy actions promoting simple interventions can save the lives of moms and babies. They wrote their own letters to Congress and tagged along as I met with people in my senators' and representatives' offices. The first time I ever met my U.S. representative, I was palm-sweating nervous. In contrast, my girls walk into a congressional office like they

---

[4]"What Have the Millennium Achievement Goals Achieved," *The Guardian*, July 6, 2015.

own the place because they've been doing it longer than they've been able to tie their shoes.

Why do my kids go to Washington with me every year? As my youngest daughter said at age nine:

> If you write a letter to Congress and just ship it out there, senators might send you a letter back saying, "I will watch this bill." But if someone comes in and physically talks to them and then hands in a bunch of letters from kids and adults and everyone is posting it on social media and everyone's agreeing with this . . . it's sort of like the senators and representatives might get in trouble if they DON'T.

By the time my kids became teenagers, they were writing letters to the editor for newspapers and training new advocates.

Walking the hallways of Capitol Hill with my children at the 2014 RESULTS International Conference and Lobby Day.

Our advocacy makes me so proud of my family. Together with my "babies," I'm changing the world for all moms and their babies. Working to save lives and raising compassionate humans is the most worthy use of my time I can imagine right now. It allows me to become a truly empowered individual and develop deeper connections with my children. It is my dearest hope that I'm empowering them as well.

Seeing Results

I have had ups and downs in my adventures as a mom-advocate. Most of the time, I'm the person cheering others on as they find their voices. On frustrating days, I need to be reminded of my impact so I can keep moving. I'll wrap up this section by describing a few of the high points that demonstrate just how far my advocacy has come since a stinky diaper made a memorable first impression on a congressional aide.

One week in the spring of 2015 was particularly full of victories. On Sunday, I learned that a long opinion piece I had written about child survival had been printed in my local paper. On Monday, I called in to a local St. Louis radio show to talk with Illinois Congressman Rodney Davis. Although I wasn't his constituent, he was visiting my state, which gave me the chance to ask him on the air to sign onto a new policy on global maternal and child health. Using practiced techniques for speaking briefly and powerfully about an issue, I convinced him to look up the policy on his phone during the interview, and he signed on just a few hours later!

On Tuesday, I got word that my own Congresswoman Ann Wagner had signed onto that same proposal. Her signature came after we had spent a year reaching out to her through meetings, published media, phone call-in days, hundreds of handwritten letters, and even children showing up with paper dolls at her local district office. On Friday, I boarded a plane to D.C. for a weekend RESULTS board retreat, where I would help lay the groundwork for empowering more activists so they could, someday, enjoy a great week like mine.

Another pivotal moment gave me concrete affirmation of how much my words matter. In 2013, Senator Dick Durbin of Illinois sent me an official copy of his speech where he recognized me and Richard Smiley by name for our work on microfinance advocacy. That speech was entered into the congressional record.

Speaking to U.S. Senator Dick Durbin with my RESULTS Chicago co-leader Richard Smiley at a Congressional Gold Medal reception honoring Professor Muhammad Yunus.

Holding the copy in my hands, I realized that all of this volunteer advocacy work had made me part of American history. The framed document hangs on my wall now, a daily reminder to myself that I have actually influenced Congress and can continue to do so every day for the rest of my life.

It's Your Turn!

1. In what ways has being a mother changed your awareness of your community and the world?
2. Do you feel more deeply connected to any issues or causes since you became a mother? If so, how?
3. What feelings and desires do you think you share with all mothers?
4. Do you want the world to be different by the time your children are grown? If so, how?
5. Think about the world during your childhood. What things are better now because people came together and spoke out for changes?

Notes

CHAPTER 2

WHAT DOES A MOM-ADVOCATE DO?

ADVOCACY CAN BE AN intimidating word that can stop a budding conversation dead in its tracks. But the concept doesn't have to be complicated or scary. As I mentioned earlier, I like to use a nice, friendly definition: expressing yourself to inspire action from another person with the power to help.

That help could come in many forms, such as a monetary donation or the changing of a law. Sometimes, advocacy involves nothing more than telling the right story to the right person at the right time. Because members of the U.S. Congress hold a lot of power to affect the issues I care about, I'm usually trying to "tell the right story" to U.S. senators and representatives.

I want to share an illustration of advocacy that I use with kids because I believe if you can explain a concept to a child, you will be better able to explain it to adults. Plus, let's face it, most of us would rather hear a child-friendly explanation of everything from the Big Bang to balancing our checkbooks.

Little Toy Clown: Hero Advocate

The Little Engine That Could, by Watty Piper, is a classic children's tale of persistence best remembered for the Little Blue Engine who chants, "I think I can. I think I can. I think I can," as she pulls toys over the hill to children waiting on the other side.[5] Little Blue, who steps in to help a stranded train of toys after larger engines have refused, is a great example I use to remind my kids to never give up.

However, my favorite character in this story is the Little Toy Clown who is rarely remembered, even though he displays at least as much persistence as Little Blue Engine. After the engine pulling the train full of toys breaks down at the foot of a tall mountain, Little Toy Clown inspires the toys to plead for help from passing engines. "'Please, oh, please, Big Engine,' cried all the dolls and toys together. 'Won't you please pull our train over the mountain?'"

Little Toy Clown waves his flag to stop each engine one-by-one with unwavering faith that he will find help for their cause. After each disappointment, he encourages the toys and keeps looking for help. "'Cheer up,' cried the little toy clown. 'The Freight Engine is not the only one in the world. Here comes another.' . . . So the little toy clown waved his flag and the dingy, rusty old engine stopped."

---

[5] Watty Piper, *The Little Engine That Could* (New York: Platt and Munk 1930).

Little Toy Clown is the true advocate of the book. He demonstrates an ideal model of advocacy when he inspires the toys to cry out together with a unified voice. After an engine refuses to help, Little Toy Clown "rallies the stakeholders" (that's organizer-speak for gathering everybody who is affected by the problem) and seeks out his next meeting to request aid from someone else with the power to help.

Little Toy Clown engages in advocacy every time he organizes the other toys or waves his flag to stop an engine to request help for himself and the other passengers. He delivers a clear request with sound reasoning behind it. In fact, Little Toy Clown is the best possible advocate. As one of the toys lacking a way over the mountain, he personally needs help, and he has a unified group behind him making their collective case. As a spokesman, Little Toy Clown can connect the immediate needs of the passengers of the stranded train to the greater needs of the children on the other side of the mountain, who wait not only for dolls and toys, but also for the fresh fruits and veggies the train is carrying. Little Toy Clown repeatedly sets up meetings with potential allies and never gives up until he finds someone to help.

So, that's what advocates do. Do you think you can do what a toy clown in a children's book can do?

I think you can. I think you can. I think you can.

Waving Our Flags

So, how do advocates in the real world raise their flags to get help for others? We do it by meeting with people we elect to Congress, getting media to cover our issues, and organizing other folks to contact Congress and the media through phone calls, emails, social media, or letters. These actions are open to all American citizens and U.S. residents, but most of us rarely take such actions because we haven't been taught how. And too few people realize our officials can be some of the engines we need to lift people over the metaphorical hills of poverty, racism, or other adversities.

Even though U.S. government classes are required in middle and high schools, many of us—including me—remember very little from those classes beyond the basic ideas that Americans have three branches of government and a bunch of rights guaranteed by the Constitution. If you're here from a different country, you might not have even been taught that much. The good news is that you don't need to be an expert in American politics to be an advocate. But it's important to know the following: each state has two elected U.S. senators representing the whole state, each state is divided into congressional districts with U.S. representatives, and each citizen is federally represented by their two senators and one representative.

The next step is to learn how you actually make your opinions and desires known to your senators and representatives. Until I became involved in advocacy, I didn't understand how citizens could influence government beyond voting and volunteering for a political campaign. I now know that we actually have many ways to effectively reach out to our government well before and well after Election Day.

We can contact congressional offices directly by mailing letters, sending emails, making phone calls, or visiting in person. We can also get government officials to pay attention to us by generating media attention—encouraging reporters to write newspaper articles about our cause or getting local radio or TV stations to cover an event or broadcast an interview. We can write our own letters and opinion pieces to be published in newspapers. Even information posted in blogs or social media can help us get our message to decision-makers.

Waving Our Mom Flags

What unique types of actions can mom-advocates take to contact Congress or educate our communities? We can:

- Read a book to preschool children about a particular issue, then help them color pictures about that topic to mail to a representative along with a note from an adult
- Help Scout troops earn a citizenship badge
- Paint a thank-you poster with children and mail it to a congressional representative
- Help a child practice penmanship by writing a short note to a senator

As a parent of a young child, you probably find yourself reading, writing, or making art on a regular basis. If you occasionally focus one of these familiar activities on an important cause and then send pictures of your kids taking part in these activities to a senator, representative, or newspaper, then those everyday parenting activities suddenly become powerful advocacy actions.

Here are other ways mom-advocates might wave their flags:

- Post information about an issue to social media while waiting to pick up kids from a class
- Email a representative from a phone while standing in line at a grocery store

- Leave a phone message for a senator while waiting for your hair appointment
- Meet another mom to talk about an issue over coffee
- Write for a church or temple newsletter on a policy affecting the congregation
- Type out a newspaper editorial on a laptop surrounded by a pile of Legos
- Gather some co-workers during a lunch break to educate them on an issue
- Handwrite letters to Congress with friends while the kids watch a movie
- Coach a group of wine-drinking friends on how to write a letter to the editor
- Stand at a podium and speak to a room full of activists
- Speak to a class of college students
- Carry a tired third-grader piggyback-style through the halls of Congress so you can be on time to meet with your representative

I know that these ideas can work because I've tried them all over the years. You might not feel ready to try some of these things and that's okay (it's true that you'll need to build up proper core strength to piggyback a nine-year-old for any significant distance). We all move in different circles and have different talents to draw upon.

But know that there are many ways to get involved, many ways to wave your mom flags and summon help for you and your fellow travelers. Just be willing to use your imagination and be persistent, and you will find help to get over the next hill.

Reverend Pamela Dolan of Davis, California made one of her first phone calls to Congress about poverty during this mom-break to get her hair done.
Photo credit: Pamela Dolan.

It's Your Turn!

1. Does the word *advocacy* intimidate you? Is it easier if you think of it as "speaking out" or "expressing your views?"
2. Is there another way to describe advocacy that feels more comfortable to you?
3. Does it surprise you that advocacy can take on many different forms, such as writing, activities with children, talking to groups, or fundraising? What other activities can advocates practice?
4. Were you involved in advocacy or other volunteer efforts before you became a mother? Could you take the same kinds of actions now? If not, what could you do instead?
5. Do any of the options for advocacy listed in this chapter sound appealing to you? Why or why not?
6. Did you learn how citizens can influence government officials during your government classes in high school or college? If so, what do you remember?

Notes

CHAPTER 3

WHY SHOULD MOMS BE ADVOCATES?

IF I SAID YOU MIGHT be the one person who could influence the actions of a U.S. senator, would that energize you? Or does that idea freak you out a little bit? By the way, it's okay to feel a little bit of both.

Why would I even suggest you might have that kind of influence? It's because you're a mom, and moms can be powerful advocates. Here are five reasons that your personal message could be more compelling than one coming from a highly paid professional lobbyist:

1. **Moms are powerful.**
2. **Moms explain things.**
3. **Moms are persistent.**
4. **Moms are responsible.**
5. **Moms are experts in the most important skills.**

Let's explore those points in more depth.

1. Moms Are Powerful

Have you ever been reduced to a weeping heap after watching a news story or a movie about children in distress? Or driven home in a haze of tears after hearing a radio update about a child in danger? In those moments, many of us think, "I wish I weren't so fragile."

Maybe you chalked up your emotional reaction to pregnancy or exhaustion from caring for your infant. Being caught up in a moment of extreme emotion can make anyone feel weak and powerless. Moms who have just given birth also get a bonus influx of oxytocin to facilitate nursing and shrinking the uterus after delivery. But oxytocin isn't nicknamed the "love" or "cuddle" hormone for nothing. It also helps transform brains to feel empathy and bond with babies.[6] New moms get a biological assist to jumpstart maternal attachment. Yet I've anecdotally observed that adoptive moms, even without the added pregnancy hormones, can feel more receptive to messages of distress from infants as well.

Chemically induced or not, maternal moments of vulnerability are precisely what give you special strength to be an advocate for those who needlessly suffer. As mothers, we often find ourselves momentarily consumed by crushing empathy when we encounter stories of parents who can't give their children what they need. But this emotional response is far from a sign of weakness. On the contrary, this ability to internalize another person's story gives you great power because caring and empathy are contagious.

---

[6] R. Feldman, A. Weller, O. Zagoory-Sharon, & A. Levine, "Evidence for a Neuroendocrinological Foundation of Human Affiliation: Plasma Oxytocin Levels Across Pregnancy and the Postpartum Period Predict Mother-Infant Bonding," *Psychological Science* (November 2007).

Take a look at this story I wrote after visiting congressional offices with Felisa Hilbert. She is a mother and a child health advocate who speaks to members of Congress and their aides many times a year, encouraging them to help save children's lives around the world.

Felisa Hilbert leans in close to congressional aides when she tells them about holding a dying infant in her arms many years ago when she was a young volunteer nurse at a small Mexican health clinic in Veracruz. As a nurse at the beginning of her career, she eagerly anticipated using her skills to help people in need.

The infant's desperate mother, who had traveled for three hours on a bus from her rural home, placed her first child in Felisa's arms saying, "Please save my kid." Felisa will never forget her face. "She had fair skin, but dark circles under her eyes. Sunken. She was thin and looked very, very sad."

The baby was perhaps twenty months old, but so very small, wearing only a cloth diaper and a tiny shirt. Like his mother, he showed signs of prolonged malnutrition. Barely breathing and very pale, the baby had suffered from diarrhea for two or three days. Hardly a fatal sentence for most children, diarrhea is a common cause of death for undernourished infants living in poverty with little access to clean water. The child felt so slight, fragile, and still that Felisa knew he was in bad shape.

"This baby is dying," she thought as she carried him to the doctor for an examination. "There is nothing we can do," he told Felisa as he handed the child back to her. It wasn't long before the baby took one last shallow breath, and Felisa had to deliver the devastating news to the exhausted mother, who now faced more heartbreak.

In the 1970s, local law required that bodies must be buried within twenty-four hours after death (this tradition is still practiced in some towns and villages today). Thus, the clinic had a legal obligation to report the passing of a patient. But that report would trigger costs for a death certificate and immediate burial because there were no funeral homes to preserve a body. The clinic staff knew this impoverished mother had spent all her money to travel to the clinic as a last-ditch attempt to save her only child. She had no money to pay for the burial. She didn't even have money for something to eat or the trip back home.

The doctor suggested that the mother wrap up the body of her child in a blanket, as if he were alive, and carry him in her arms for the return bus trip. There, she could honor her son as best she could with her family. The doctor and nurses raised funds among themselves to provide the mother with a meal and a bus ticket.

Decades passed, but the memory remained fresh for Felisa. Her voice thick with emotion, Felisa recalled the injustice of that situation. She imagined the mother riding the bus and pretending her baby was sleeping, hiding her terrible secret as she cradled what had once been her living child. "Sometimes I wish I knew how to find her and ask her how she did it. Now that I am a mother, I know I would have been crying so hard if that were my baby. She had to be stoic and brave, not even able to cry because someone might ask her questions."

The experience left a lasting brand on Felisa's heart, guiding her choices for the rest of her life. "I just felt so powerless," she remembered. "I made a promise to myself that I would do everything in my power to not let another child die from lack of such simple resources."

What feelings stirred as you read Felisa's story? Helplessness? Sadness? Anger at the injustice? Perhaps you even felt a physical reaction like a tightening in your chest or tears welling up in your eyes? Any of those emotions are valid reactions that can be used as a force for good. If you respond to a story with emotion, you will retell it with passion.

Your passion can incite a riot of emotion and resolve in your audience even if—especially if—your voice cracks. If you are addressing a senator, a congressional aide, or anyone in the path of power, you are in a position to create change. Your sincere expression is more likely to inspire action than a dry recitation of facts and figures.

Your vulnerability can be your strength. And the ability to turn your emotion into positive, constructive action can be your superpower. As a new mom, your newfound capacity to love can make you feel weak, vulnerable, and out of control at times. Yet you can turn this "weakness" into your greatest asset by becoming an advocate for people and issues you care about. Your strength comes from your motherhood.

You don't have to be a mother to feel empathetic, protective, and passionate about helping others. But many women—like me—find those emotions are awakened or strengthened in the tender moments of baby-play and the desperate moments of sleep deprivation. And once they are ignited, you might find yourself coming alive with a newfound resolve to fight for a cause.

Story time!

Katie Kraft discovered how experiences of childbirth and mother-hood added deeper meaning to her work helping mothers around the world. As a 24-year-old, she felt very fortunate to work with the United Methodist Church on global maternal mortality issues. It was her job to educate church leaders about families in poverty at risk of losing mothers during childbirth. Even though she was passionate about helping moms and infants, as a single young woman, she struggled to make the statistics real for her audiences. "I was always reaching for how to pull the emotion into it. How do I make it feel accessible and not just something that happens to people 'over there' in developing nations?" she recalls.

Later, as Katie looked forward to starting a family with her husband, tragedy struck in her own life. Just five months before she became pregnant, her mother died unexpectedly. Plus, gestational diabetes and dangerously high blood pressure put her pregnancy at risk. As time grew near for Katie to deliver, her blood pressure rose to stroke levels. "It was very touch and go, and very scary," she admits. As emergency medical staff rushed into her room, she was painfully aware of what it meant for a family to lose a mother. Thankfully, Katie had access to excellent care and survived the ordeal with her daughter, although she continued to mourn for her own mom.

When she returned to work, Katie found her harrowing experience gave her a new perspective on the information she had been presenting for six years. Along with a renewed dedication to her cause, she brought back new ways to tell the story of maternal mortality. "I was willing to be more vulnerable and emotional in the way that I talked about the future of girls and moms in society."

Katie went on to become the Deputy Director of Advocate Engagement at CARE, a poverty-fighting organization known for its focus on women and girls. Even years later, Katie's eyes welled up with bright tears when she remembered those pivotal months. "These experiences of losing my mom, becoming pregnant, and going through a high-risk birth—I'll be committed to these issues for the rest of my life."

If you respond to a random news story with an unexpected flood of painful tears, just think of it as "superpower growing pains." Your heart and empathy are growing to match what you will need to raise your child. You can even regard these bouts of compassion as birth pains. Only this time, it is you who will be born as a great agent of change to protect your child and many others.

You might be thinking that all this talk about power is great, but you have no idea how to harness your weepy moments into actions that bring about real change. What in the world would you say to a member of Congress? What good would that do anyway?

I'm going to let you in on the big secret: To be a powerful activist, your main job is to put yourself forward and say, "I care!"

Yes, educating yourself about your subject is important, and knowing key facts can definitely help make your case. Yet the emotion in your voice and body language will convey more about how much you care than the actual words you use. As the oft-quoted saying goes, people will remember how you made them feel long after they have forgotten what you said.

When you learn to combine your emotions with information and clear requests, you become dangerous to the status quo. You threaten systems that keep families stuck in cycles of suffering. And that is a very, very good thing.

2. Moms Explain Things

If you can sit on the floor and explain a concept to a second grader, then you are speaking plainly and clearly enough to be understood by a member of Congress. That may sound like a joke, but it's true. Explaining concepts to kids means boiling your message down to its most basic parts and delivering it in an engaging way. Even though U.S. representatives might sit in high-level security briefings all day, that doesn't mean they immediately understand acronyms and internal jargon or relish listening to someone reel off a bunch of numbers out of context. Children love to hear clear explanations accompanied by really good stories, and so do adult decision-makers. Never forget that they are as human as anyone else.

Fred Rogers, host of the children's television program *Mr. Rogers' Neighborhood*, knew this very well when he testified before the Senate Subcommittee on Communications in an attempt to ward off a $20 million funding cut for PBS back in 1969. The chairman, Senator John Pastore, made for a stern audience but was won over when Mr. Rogers explained what his children's program did for young viewers. Video footage of the testimony shows Mr. Rogers addressing the subcommittee in the same soothing tones he used when addressing his TV audience of preschoolers. He wasn't condescending; he was simply unhurried and calm as he explained things in a very easy-to-understand way, even reciting the words to a song he used on the program.

When Mr. Rogers patiently described the way he gave expressions of care to each child by saying "I like you just the way you are," Senator Pastore confessed, "I'm supposed to be a pretty tough guy, and this is the first time I've had goosebumps for the last two days." And after hearing Mr. Rogers give a heartfelt recitation of the lyrics to "What do you do with the mad that you feel?" Pastore declared, "I think it's wonderful. Looks like you just earned the 20 million dollars."[7]

Of course, I'm not advising you to use a sing-songy preschool voice for adults; just speak plainly and get to the point. Most aides and legislators truly appreciate a polite constituent who can do exactly that.

 Tips and Ideas

Tips for using mom-skills to communicate

Whether explaining things to children or senators, I find it's best to prepare a talk as if I'm getting ready for a Scout troop meeting. I always try to:

- Be brief
- Speak in plain language
- Tell a story to illustrate the important point
- Clearly tell your listeners what they should do
- Be prepared for some random interruptions
- Be prepared to use a different way to tell the audience what they should do if they don't understand your first take

3. Moms Are Persistent

It would be nice to think that our government is such a well-oiled machine that it only takes one conversation to convince a

---

[7] Fred Rogers, testimony, U.S. Senate Subcommittee on Communications, May 1, 1969.

policymaker to support your request. In reality, it usually takes time, patience, and more reminders than you give your children to get their laundry off the floor.

Unfortunately, no matter how urgent you feel your issue is, there will always be hundreds of other matters clamoring for a congressperson's attention. Plus, if the office staffers are not already aware of your issue, they're going to have to research and consider your request even if they don't oppose it. A mother's touch to provide helpful information and consistent reminders is an incredible advantage.

A heaping helping of persistence is often needed to get your request noticed by a senator or representative. There's a good reason that aides are referred to as "gatekeepers." They decide what to put in front of their boss and when. Favorite issues brought by favored lobbyists might get fast-tracked immediately. I've been in that position before. *Whee!* It's like riding the "ice cream float" card up toward the finish line in the Candyland board game! Thorny issues brought by unfamiliar lobbyists might get stranded on the bottom of the pile for a long time. I've been there, too. *Boo!* That's like getting trapped in Candyland's "molasses swamp." If you're stuck in the swamp, you can pull out the bag of tricks you use when your children are dawdling. You know how to keep prodding and still keep your mommy cool.

Even when you receive an immediate "yes" from a member of Congress, it can still take a surprising amount of follow-up communication to make sure your request is not forgotten. Maybe the bill didn't get signed because a detail just slipped somebody's mind. It could be that the congressional office team is overworked and understaffed. Some offices are just managed better than others.

Occasionally, the delay may not be the fault of your member's office. Once, I found out my senator and his aides had done everything correctly to sign on to a proposal, but their email had been lost by another senator's office! Repeatedly expressing a sense of urgency while maintaining a patient mom-face is a skill you can definitely translate to congressional use in times like these.

4. Moms Are Responsible

Once you've been the sole person standing between a happy family and total family chaos, you start to view your place in the world a little differently. Granted, many moms are fortunate to have very responsible spouses who shoulder a lot of familial tasks. But as Bill and Melinda Gates noted in their 2016 annual foundation letter, women in every part of the world—including the United States—bear the heavier responsibility for household chores and child-rearing work. Generally, moms are the ones making lunches, outfitting diaper bags, scheduling play dates, and making sure you don't run out of toilet paper or cheese sticks.

Moms of young children are chess players looking two, three, and four moves into the future. My husband is a prince among men, but even he would admit that I've always been better at heading off the tantrum before it ever starts. Why? Because I do it more often, so it has become a habit. After a while, it's second nature to expend a little bit of energy on preparation rather than to let things spin out of control later.

On my Ugandan trip, with the UN Foundation and seven other moms of young kids, a member of the media team came down with a nasty head cold as we arrived in a rural area, far from anything like a Walgreens where we could pick up some NyQuil. By morning, word spread through our group that our communications specialist wasn't doing well.

To everyone's amusement, we moms arrived at breakfast with travel-sized offerings of cold medicine and vitamin C packets from our private stashes which we reverently delivered to her table before serving ourselves. The super-moms on this trip were prepared for anything—we even had emergency rehydration salts just in case someone was literally dying of thirst!

So, how does a responsible nature translate to successful advocacy? It allows you to stay organized and prepared to respond to the needs of your volunteer groups. It gets you to meetings on time with all the materials you need. It helps you respond to emails from congressional aides in a timely manner. Moms are welcomed at advocacy conferences nationwide because of our reputation as low-maintenance, responsible, capable people, who get things done.

5. Moms Are Experts in the Most Important Skills

I'm not going to tell you that everything I needed to know about advocacy I learned in kindergarten. After all, composing and addressing letters came much later in my public education. But I insist that the most critical lessons were learned around age five, especially since the most successful advocacy usually involves teamwork. Advocates should always be prepared to:

- Treat others with kindness and respect
- Share
- Give everyone in the group a turn to play
- Avoid calling anyone a hurtful name
- Apologize when you hurt someone

◅ Say "please" and "thank you" (this is the number-one lesson and the step that is most often forgotten when talking with members of Congress as well as other volunteers)

Moms keep all of these skills top-of-mind because we coach our kids to use them every day. It has been easy for me to follow these simple and important rules in my advocacy efforts because I tend to bring my children along to volunteer gatherings and congressional meetings. Of course, I want to model good behavior for my kids when they are present. We know these rules inside and out and should be able to follow them even when our children aren't in the same room. We can model these important skills for young college activists and aging senators alike.

Our mommy voices especially need to be heard today in our political climate of nastiness that permeates cable news and social media. If you watch only TV news, you might think that yelling and insulting each other is normal for anyone who works on Capitol Hill. Well, it isn't. That is behavior the networks highlight in order to boost ratings. Professional business still happens there every day, carried out by real humans who want to be treated with respect. Moms can be at the forefront of carrying a positive tone of reason, kindness, and civility into D.C.

It's Your Turn!

1. What issues tug at your heartstrings most? What are you most passionate about?
2. What would you change about the world if you could—no matter how big or small—for your child and all children?
3. Can you think of a time when someone told you a story that saddened or uplifted you? Why do you think it stuck with

you? What was it about the story or storyteller that resonated with you?

4.   Have you experienced a moment of unexpected, heightened emotion because of hormones, lack of sleep, or stress related to caring for a child? Describe that moment. Why do you think it affected you so deeply?

5.   Can you think of instances where you set a good example with your patience and politeness while having to repeatedly remind someone (child or adult) to complete a task?

6.   What other "kindergarten manners" would be useful in relating to members of Congress and other volunteers?

7.   Can you think of other "mommy traits" that might be helpful in convincing people to understand your point of view?

Notes

Columba Sainz

Photo credit: Karina Córdova.

CHAPTER 4

PROFILE: COLUMBA SAINZ INTERLOCKING ISSUES

SOCIAL ISSUES TEND TO be presented like competing problems we're supposed to work on separately. In reality, most people experience layers of interrelated problems. Columba Sainz's story of environmental activism demonstrates how pollution, poverty, race, immigration, health issues, and even transportation problems combine to make life difficult for families.

While raising two young girls and a baby boy in Phoenix, Columba has struggled to improve her family's health. Only two months after moving from Tucson in 2018, Columba's two-year-old daughter, who had no known medical issues, started wheezing at night and feeling very ill. Doctors prescribed asthma medicine without hesitation, but Columba was uneasy about the side effects of constant medication and wondered if something in the environment was causing such a sudden onset of symptoms.

She soon began worrying about the health of the rest of her family. Her four-year-old daughter developed respiratory problems as well. Columba became horribly sick during her entire pregnancy with her son. Researching her family's personal health mystery, she learned that other families like hers were also suffering. "That's when I discovered that a majority of Latino children [in Phoenix] have asthma in comparison to white people. I started to connect all the dots. If I live here, who else lives here? Who can afford to live here? What's happening in my surroundings?"

Columba discovered her family was living in an air pollution "hot spot" in downtown Phoenix, where emissions from specific sources expose the population to high risks of adverse health effects. Busy freeways surrounded her home in one of the fastest-growing counties in the country. Two huge nearby parking lots housed city and school buses each night, creating concentrated sources of diesel fumes as the buses left and returned each day. And she was only five minutes away from the busy Phoenix Sky Harbor International Airport, ranked thirteenth for traffic in the U.S.

"On top of that, the topography of this area is like a big bowl combining it all with high heat," she explained. Each July, Phoenix averages a daily maximum temperature between 104 and 107 degrees Fahrenheit. "In the summer, we have constant high polluted days. So, me taking my daughter to the park right in front of my house for two or three hours was the worst thing I could do as a mother."

Data from the American Lung Association's 2020 State of the Air report aligned with Columba's experience.[8] It ranked the

---

[8] American Lung Association, "Most Polluted Cities," https://www.stateoftheair.org/.

Phoenix area as having some of the worst air in the country. Specifically, Maricopa County—where Columba's family continues to live—received an F grade with far more alert days for high levels of harmful ground-level ozone than anywhere else in Arizona.

Although Columba was not sure how to use this information to help protect her family, she was well aware of the power of Congress to address problems like pollution. Working with Mi Familia Vota, a civic engagement organization, she understood how to unite communities to elect candidates for change. But the idea of working on legislation with lawmakers was new to her until she learned about Moms Clean Air Force, an organization of over 1,000,000 parent activists with a mission to protect children from air pollution and climate change.

Columba shared their vision for a safe, stable, and equitable future where all children breathe clean air. With them, she learned to speak from her heart to advocate with lawmakers for just and healthy solutions to air pollution. Those in-person conversations with parents were critical to convincing legislators to take action.

"We go to meetings not as experts or scientists, but as moms," Columba explained. "As moms, we know the impacts on our children."

Columba shows elected officials how seemingly separate issues overlap. She wasn't aware of the hot spot phenomenon when she was looking for a home, but low housing prices suggest the real estate industry had a good idea something undesirable was happening there. The polluted area is home primarily to people of color, which means the neighborhood's pollution problems feed racial injustice. And because those living in the hot spot are low-income residents, they are less likely to have good health insurance or adequate resources to cope with the health challenges caused by the pollution.

For example, filtered air conditioning in a hot Arizona summer provides indoor relief, but it's a financial burden many can't afford. Columba affirmed, "A bill of electricity [with air-conditioning] is really expensive. Sometimes it's the same amount you would pay for a one-bedroom apartment. Imagine having no work during the pandemic summer of 2020, having no health insurance, and having asthma without air conditioning in your house."

Even worse than the lack of funds for air conditioning is the lack of healthcare. Columba advocates alongside families who don't have money to cover an emergency visit without insurance.

In addition, the immigrant population worries about confrontations over citizenship. Columba encountered a little girl whose single father was undocumented. She tried to keep her asthma in check just by sheer will alone to protect him.

"I don't know how this kid did it!" Columba marveled. "When she had an asthma attack, she would do her best to control herself. Sometimes our children are afraid to go to an E.R. because we are afraid that they will ask, 'Where are your papers? Where is your social security?' I think that's horrible, you know? When you need to go to the emergency room, you need to go. When you don't have the papers, they won't take care of you because they know they can't charge anyone for the medical assistance. And it's expensive. It's really, really expensive."

Today, Columba and her family live ten minutes outside of the downtown Phoenix area where they suffered so many health problems. Even such a small distance makes a significant improvement in air quality. Yet she continues to work with mothers in places where she used to live and keeps their stories close to her heart. Once she met a desperate mom who was running away from one area to help her child with severe respiratory issues. But she stopped to rest in a park in the hot spot, which was worse. It was as if that mother was running from an invisible monster with no idea which way to turn.

"She had everything in her car," Columba remembered. "She said, 'I drove all the way here because I thought I was going to find clean air. And now I don't know where to go. Can you tell me where to go? Do you know where the air is clean?' Her story was even worse than mine . . . like life or death. That's the desperation of a mother who has been exposed to air pollution."

"What gives me the fuel to do this with all my heart," Columba insisted, "is that, as a mother, I want my children to grow connecting with nature. I keep doing it because I want my children to be able to breathe clean air. We have data that agrees that if we don't take action in thirty-five years, we're going to be living with a lot of things we don't want. We're living with them even now! I want to leave a better planet for my children's children."

Notes

CHAPTER 5

WHAT DIFFERENCE CAN ONE MOM MAKE?

IMAGINE YOU ARE HAVING a picnic near the banks of a raging river. You hear a cry for help and see several people—men, women, and children—fighting for their lives in the middle of the current. Mothers try to hold their babies above the water, but they are drowning. Children are being sucked under with exhausted parents.

You and your fellow picnickers jump into action, tossing ropes and floats into the raging waters to reach as many people as you can, one by one. The survivors are grateful, but they point upriver to show you even more victims swept helplessly along. Maybe you and your shore-side buddies devise a brilliant system of ropes and pulleys to rescue multiple people, but there are far too many to save.

While your party is fishing people out of the water, you turn your eyes upriver and wonder, "Why is this happening? Did a bridge collapse? Is there someone pushing people in the river? Is there some terrible danger up there that makes a perilous plunge the better choice?"

You travel upstream to find a way to prevent people from falling into the river in the first place. Because you are a change-focused advocate, you decide to find the root cause of the suffering and strategically use your influence to eliminate that cause so that *no one* has to drown. Once you figure out a strategy to save the most people, you will share it and convince your community to follow your plan.

Direct Service Versus Advocacy

The river scenario illustrates the difference between "direct service" and "advocacy." Direct service workers give of their energy and talents to help people in moments of need. Disaster relief workers, soup kitchen servers, and polio vaccinators are examples of direct service providers. On-the-ground relief work can be incredibly satisfying as it connects volunteers directly to individuals who need help. Most people think about direct service when they think about volunteering and charity work.

Change advocates take a wider approach and use their voices to rally even more help for the long term. At its best, advocacy is about seeking out root causes, finding effective solutions, and persuading other people to help implement those solutions. The work can feel far removed from the people you are trying to help, which some find less rewarding than direct service roles.

Working to change a system requires an ability to delay the natural human desire for instant gratification and personal words of thanks. But when you are successful, when you know that no more people will fall into the metaphorical river or—in the real world—that we are 99% of the way to eradicating polio, then it feels very, very gratifying to know that you saved many more people than you ever could have if you never took the mental leap to leave the riverbank.

Serving Millions, not Hundreds

My decision to move upstream in the fight against hunger in America came after my children were born. As a busy mom, I have learned to continually ask myself, "Since I'm just one person, how can I make the most difference with the limited time and energy I have to volunteer?"

When I was childless and single with lots of free time, I served dinner regularly in a church soup kitchen. Standing behind serving tables, scooping casserole, and welcoming the hundreds of people who streamed into the great hall became a highlight of my month. It warmed my heart to hear their words of thanks and to see children happily munching the dessert I put on their plates. I drove home knowing people had full bellies because of those hours I had volunteered with fellow congregants.

Over time, I started to worry about what soup kitchen clients did on days when they couldn't get hot meals from the church. So, I moved a little farther upstream and began volunteering with the Greater Chicago Food Depository packaging food for pantries all around the area. Although I felt like my work was making a difference, my personal efforts seemed dwarfed by the immense need in the echoing warehouse. Unfortunately, even those efforts ended after my first baby was born. I had to step away from those hands-on projects as neither were compatible with the hands-on work required for baby care.

Eventually, I learned from Bread for the World that I didn't have to give up the battle against hunger even if I could no longer spend hours in a soup kitchen or food pantry. In fact, the work I had been doing only addressed a symptom—hunger—without addressing its root cause—poverty. Lack of a living wage, mass incarceration, lack of affordable housing, and even food subsidies in the U.S. Farm Bill all play a part in perpetuating a cycle of poverty resulting in hunger.

To truly help more people, I could use my voice to change the systems and policies that perpetuate hunger. Plus, I could pursue that work even while caring for my small children. Of course, moving my efforts further up the river would mean that I would never meet most of the people who would benefit from my work, and I would rarely hear personal expressions of gratitude.

Not everyone has the patience for congressional work, but I soon discovered I was okay with it. I realized advocacy was the best place for my personal gifts.

Both Roles Are Vital

Even if you prefer to work as a direct service provider, you'll probably find it satisfying to take a simple advocacy action now and then, such as writing to Congress or signing an online petition. You could also team up with an advocate who is working on a similar issue. Advocates can set up meetings with elected officials, write newspaper pieces, or arrange for public awareness events that create opportunities for direct service volunteers to tell their stories to the right people at the right time.

Similarly, being an advocate does not mean you can never be involved in direct service. Hands-on work frequently provides inspiration and personal stories to fuel advocacy. You don't have to choose one or the other!

Food donations *and* better government policies are needed to feed our communities, so we need direct service providers *and* advocates to solve the complicated problem of hunger—and many others like it.

RESULTS advocates taking a turn at direct service by packing food to be shipped to people in need with St. Louis World Food Day.

⏱ Story 📖 time!

The first time I personally played a part in saving millions of lives through advocacy, I could hardly believe it.

I reread my own email a hundred times. It began with "Dear Congresswoman" and ended with my phone number. In between, it asked her to sign on to the "Tom Lantos and Henry J. Hyde United States Global Leadership Against HIV/AIDS, Tuberculosis, and Malaria Reauthorization Act of 2008."

The email could not have been over one hundred words long and the name of the bill was about twenty percent of the content! The complicated name made me nervous even though I had learned from several training sessions how the bill would help battle three deadly diseases that decimated so many families in extreme poverty. The bill authorized the release of $48 billion over five years for AIDS, tuberculosis, and malaria programs. Millions of people would be cured or protected from illness if it passed.

I included an invitation for the congresswoman to call me if she had questions, although I felt queasy about the idea of speaking one-on-one to someone in power. I hit the *send* button and told myself no one was likely to even read this, much less call back.

A day later, my cell phone rang, and an unfamiliar number popped on my screen. A very professional-sounding woman introduced herself as the foreign policy aide to my congresswoman. She thanked me for my email and informed me that Congresswoman Schakowsky would be signing on to the bill because of my request. She wished me a good day and invited me to keep in touch.

When she hung up, I stared at the phone, dumbfounded, still not believing what had just happened. Then I started to smile. I *did* that! Who had the power? Me!

I jumped up and started flapping my arms in an exuberantly silent chicken dance. It was the only way I could release my exhilarating energy without waking the children from their naps!

Working Upstream: The Power of Advocacy

Sadly, the world rarely protects its poorest children without advocacy. But they receive help today because thousands of everyday people like you and me pressure decision-makers to save the lives of the most vulnerable.

While attending a ONE Moms Campaign conference about issues of girls and women in poverty, I had the opportunity to hear *New York Times* columnist Nicholas Kristof. When I asked him about the power of advocacy, he replied that a small group of constituents can be particularly effective when they focus on a nonpartisan issue that is not well known. He explained it using an example of RESULTS volunteers who successfully advocate for global tuberculosis program funding. He said,

> Nobody is against funding for tuberculosis. Nobody thinks about it. So, if a modest number of calls is made to a congressman's office asking, "Where do you stand on TB funding?" when he hasn't got any calls in the other direction, he has no idea where he stands on TB funding. It's easier for him to make that move.

I was glad he told that story because this has been my experience as well. I focus most of my attention and advocacy efforts on child health. Some aspects of that broad issue, like gun violence, can unfortunately become partisan or controversial. Yet most of the time, if we concentrate on the well-being of children and remain persistent, we can find common ground to work with our members of Congress.

It is immensely satisfying to know that the world has made real and glorious progress in child health. Worldwide, the mortality rate for children under five dropped by almost sixty percent in almost thirty years—from ninety-three deaths per 1,000 live births in 1990 to thirty-eight in 2019.[9] Back then, more than 30,000 children a day died from treatable and preventable causes. In 2019, that number was down to 14,247 a day.

The progress represents the hard work and endless persistence of citizen activists who channeled their loving care for children into advocacy and convinced governments to fund large-scale efforts to eradicate disease and improve living conditions.

Although child death rates dropped dramatically, 5.3 million children under five years old still died from mostly preventable diseases in 2018. Plus, the COVID-19 virus greatly impeded access to health care for all children after its appearance in 2020. It may take years to accurately evaluate the impact of the pandemic on child survival rates. So we cannot give up. A world with zero deaths from preventable diseases is possible in our generation if we can unite our leaders to address the problems.

When my kids were little, I sat them on my lap and shared my vision that the world could be free of such suffering for children. Someday, I may talk to future grandchildren and tell them how hard we worked to finally end the senseless deaths of children

---

[9] UNICEF report, "Levels & Trends in Child Mortality, Report 2020, Estimates developed by the UN Inter-agency Group for Child Mortality Estimation."

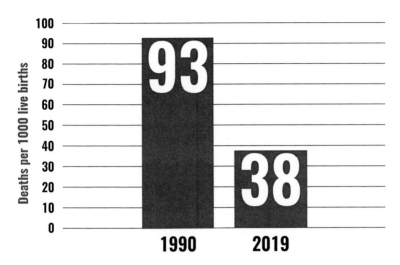

Under-Five Mortality Rate

*Data from UNICEF-2020-Child-Mortality-Report.pdf, "Levels & Trends in Child Mortality, Report 2020, Estimates developed by the UN Inter-agency Group for Child Mortality Estimation"

around the world. This is possible with the love, optimism, and strategy put into action by everyday citizens who dare to speak out.

The Power of One

In the advocacy world, the right person making a request can make all the difference. I saw this firsthand when I lobbied with RESULTS about the issue of microfinance. Microfinance involves very small loans granted to people in poverty so that a borrower can make an investment (like the purchase of a sewing machine or farm equipment) to create a business and lift themselves out of poverty with dignity.

My team of Chicago volunteers visited an aide for Congressman Peter Roskam of Illinois, requesting his signature on a resolution supporting microfinance. The aide was kind enough to grant us a meeting although we didn't have anyone on our team from his area. He listened politely to our presentation and then told us his boss would only consider such a request from a constituent, someone who actually lived in the district he represented. Even though the congressman had taken trips to developing countries to visit microfinance programs and was generally supportive of them, he put a very high value on listening to the people he was elected to represent.

We left the office to consider the challenge and brainstorm a solution in the hallway. I recalled that I once had been seated at a dinner event with Sandra Joireman of Bread for the World who lived in Roskam's district. Standing in the hallway, I called Sandra, who readily agreed to call the aide and make the request by phone. Mere days later, I got a call confirming that the congressman had signed on to the bill. Hooray for networking and the power of a single constituent!

What if *you* are the constituent in your district with the right request, at the right time, for your member of Congress? You could be the one person who can make the difference for your state!

The Power of Many

Our government operates on highly partisan lines these days, and I admit that it is much harder to influence your congressional representatives on highly visible, controversial issues on which they've already taken a strong position. It takes much more than one voice to sway elected officials away from a position clearly defined by their party. Yet when a mom decides to draw the attention of many to those issues, she can make a huge difference in her world and her community by providing the vision for others to follow.

For hot-button issues, a successful strategy is to gather enough supporters around you to become increasingly hard to ignore. Leaders of Moms Demand Action for Gun Sense in America have figured this out. I went to my first St. Louis area Moms Demand meeting because my friend wanted to participate and thought my presence would help her feel comfortable in such a small group setting. That meeting consisted of only a handful of people in a modest-sized library room. A couple of years and several horrible mass shootings later, their numbers swelled to a size requiring them to meet in large capacity church sanctuaries and branch out new chapters within the Greater St. Louis area.

Now, hundreds of mothers and allies from all over the state wear distinctive "Moms Demand" red shirts to our state capital of Jefferson City on annual advocacy days. On those days, our Missouri state legislators know exactly who is coming to visit. These moms have, indeed, become very hard to ignore.

Volunteer advocates at the first Moms Demand Advocacy Day in Jefferson City, Missouri, in February 2016.
Photo by Becky Morgan.

Volunteer advocates at the annual Moms Demand Advocacy Day in Jefferson City, Missouri in February 2020.
Photo by Becky Morgan.

It's Your Turn!

1. Have you done direct service volunteer work in the past? If so, what did you do? Has becoming a mom has changed your ability to continue those volunteer efforts?

2. What issues are you most concerned about today in the world or in your local community? What do you think are the root causes of those issues?

3. Could better laws or government policies improve the problems you see? If you don't know, are there advocacy organizations that can help you find out?

4. What are some issues, big or small, that you or people you know have advocated for at your children's school, in your neighborhood, or in your town? Do your kids advocate to you

at home, such as when you discuss family chore assignments or screen time?

5. An individual donation of $20 can provide life-saving vaccinations against measles, polio, pneumococcal virus, and rotavirus to one child. The U.S. government regularly gives over $200 million for global immunization programs. Would you prefer to a) donate your own money to save a small number of infants, b) donate your time to ask Congress for funding increases to save hundreds of thousands more infants per year, or both? Why?

Felisa Hilbert

Photo provided by Felisa Hilbert.

CHAPTER 6

PROFILE: FELISA HILBERT GROWING YOUR IMPACT

LOVE RADIATES FROM FELISA Hilbert the moment she enters a room. Whether she's greeting a child waiting for a medical test, an old friend, or a congressional aide, her sparkling eyes convey joy in their presence. Her diminutive four-foot-eleven-inch frame barely contains her enthusiasm to connect with others. A nurse by training, former missionary from the Church of Jesus Christ of Latter-day Saints, mother to three adult children, founder of a rural medical clinic, and passionate advocate for moms and children, Felisa is always ready to share a smile and a story.

Felisa has been helping others and speaking out her entire life. Even while growing up in Mexico, she felt an innate sense of duty to do everything she could to serve.

"Mom said I was the kind of child that was very observant and would see things in a different way. I gave my shoes to someone because they didn't have shoes and there was going to be a parade. I didn't understand why I had shoes and someone else did not," Felisa said. "Mom was mad."

Because of her energy, excitement, and outspokenness, friends and teachers described Felisa as a "firecracker" in school. Her father died when she was nine years old, but not before he passed on his belief in her potential to make a mark on the world. "I learned very early from my father that I can do anything. He told me, 'One person can make an impact and size doesn't have anything do with it.'"

After graduating from college in Mexico, Felisa raised her kids with Dan, her American husband, in multiple states in the U.S. before she settled in Oklahoma in 1998. She knows firsthand the difficulties immigrant parents face when they are raising children and how frustrating it can be to struggle with a new language. When she saw how parents' lack of English skills were becoming barriers to their children's educational success, Felisa organized programs through the local Parent Teacher Association (PTA) to meet the needs of minority families. Through the PTA, she connected with Parenting Magazine's Mom Congress, a U.S. mother's rights organization focused on policy issues of motherhood and education.

The highlight of her Mom Congress experience was a trip to Washington, D.C., where Felisa visited congressional offices and met U.S. Secretary of Education Arne Duncan face-to-face. She discovered those national meetings could be more effective in making change on a big scale than her local work. "I was fascinated that they wanted to hear my opinions, out-of-the-box ideas, and different perspectives. I got hooked! I wanted to learn everything

I could to be a better advocate. I started writing to my legislators, visiting their offices, and writing letters to the editor."

With these newfound skills, she considered the plight of Mexican children in poverty and turned her sights to international aid. She began lifting her voice with advocacy groups like Shot@Life and RESULTS for global vaccine funding. Her heartfelt anecdotes and positive personality made her a welcome visitor in the offices of senators and representatives.

At the same time, she longed to do something more tangible to help in her home country. In 2014, on a trip to teach advocacy skills to local leaders in Mexico, she met an Indigenous community in the Zongolica Mountains of Veracruz, Mexico. Forty families struggled in poverty largely because of their remote location. They spoke only Nahuatl, a language of the Aztecs. Even though the leaders of the community were men, she sought the opinions of women who were not speaking. She told her interpreter, "I want the moms. I want to hear what they have to say. If they had a wish, what would they want?" Won over by her sincerity and warmth, the moms told her stories about their children dying without proper medical care. They wanted a health clinic.

She dedicated herself to becoming as much a part of the community as possible during spring, summer, and Christmas visits. She explained her philosophy of engagement by saying, "I love to be with people. I don't like to be over there looking like I'm just here to teach. I like to be working with them, sitting on the floor eating with them, and knowing them. I don't want to be the big savior."

Using input from the whole community, Felisa developed plans and budgets. Inspired by her relationships, she set out to raise $10,000 as a start for their little clinic. She sold 500 tamales, hosted restaurant fundraisers, sold handcrafted jewelry, and even sold off her good jewelry and other valuables out of her own home to fund the endeavor. By 2016, she opened the doors to the clinic, Casa de Salud Tetzilquila.

Felisa visited as often as possible to take part in providing routine immunizations and free, basic medical care. Memories of patients at the clinic became powerful narratives that helped members of Congress understand how even modest foreign aid investments can transform the lives of actual people.

One of the success stories Felisa tells is about her 2019 trip when she brought her usual number of forty toys and forty goody bags to give to the children. She was surprised to learn that she should have brought far more! The number of children being served by the clinic had doubled because of improved survival from the immunizations and basic care they were receiving.

"What a wonderful problem to have!" Felisa said. "Children were growing and even going to an elementary school with a bilingual teacher speaking Spanish and Nahuatl."

To Felisa, her work at the clinic and her activism are two parts of the same mission. She knows the value of the direct service she provides with the clinic, and she's also aware that advocacy multiplies her personal influence many times over.

"Being an advocate can change not only one community, but many communities by taking one action. Why stop with one community when you can reach more and have a bigger impact? Maybe you will never know how many people you'll help . . . it doesn't matter. The important thing is that kids are getting better lives."

Notes

"Each meeting with Congress makes me feel really empowered and confident. Like I can do this, but not just this . . . I can do life."
—**Candace Ellis,** Belleville, IL

"I think even a small thing like writing a letter is changing from being passive and negative to active and positive."
—**Helena Webb,** St. Louis, Missouri

"It makes me feel like a better mom—as if I've done something to impact their future that didn't include a potty or snack food. It also makes me feel in control of something bigger than myself and I love the example that it sets for those around me, including my kids!"
—**Jennifer DeFranco,** Palatine, Illinois

"Taking action brings me peace."
—**Cara Fleischer,** Tallahassee, Florida

"I feel like I'm making a difference and even if it is a small difference, it makes me proud. Proud to be a mom, an educator, and a citizen."
—**Lisa Turner Sahadevan,** Atlanta, Georgia

"I feel like I am deserving of the space I inhabit on this Earth. I am worthy of being here . . . especially when my actions help others who are unable to act."
—**Liessa Alperin,** Ballwin, Missouri

CHAPTER 7

CAN ADVOCACY MAKE YOUR LIFE BETTER?

AS YOU THINK ABOUT jumping into advocacy, it makes sense to consider the question, "What is in it for me?"

Doing good for others should not equal martyrdom. Moms already give so much of themselves to their families every single day. You are entitled to get something in return—and advocacy has a lot to offer!

I frequently talk to moms after they take an advocacy action, and most tell me their actions bring feelings of pride, satisfaction, and self-worth. Although most people worry that becoming an advocate will just add more stress to their busy lives, moms who engage in advocacy tell me they feel more control and less anxiety.

Such positive benefits can absolutely transform your life in the long run. When you make room for activism, you:

1. **Define yourself.** Advocacy can shape you into someone who increases the good in the world. Taking a stand for my beliefs helped me become someone I'm proud to be.

2. **Engage your brain.** Thinking beyond a daily routine of childcare has positive benefits for both your present and your future. Advocacy can help you explore ideas that take you beyond your daily duties. It can even allow you to hone professional skills and build your résumé.

3. **Choose your own destiny.** If you're not intentional about how you spend your time, you may end up doing a lot of busy-work for someone else. A mindful advocate can set aside time to shape her world.

4. **Deepen friendships.** When moms take actions together, they create much stronger bonds than when they sit at the playground rehashing the same kid-related topics. Like-minded advocates often cultivate great friendships through thoughtful conversations.

5. **Empower yourself.** Seeing proof that your actions matter will make you feel more powerful. Every mother, no matter where she lives in the world, feels stronger and more confident when she sees evidence of her own influence.

Let's explore these ideas further.

1. Define Yourself

When a woman first becomes a mom, she's faced with the exciting and sometimes overwhelming task of reinventing her self-image as she takes on an entirely new physical and emotional challenge. Even a professional leader, at the top of her game, must come to terms with being a novice at motherhood. It can eat away at anyone's confidence.

Whether or not a new mom is employed, her situation changes. She thinks about herself differently. Some moms keep their jobs, shifting between work and home identities. Some easily and happily make the transition to caring for a child 24/7. Others find themselves in an unfamiliar social or professional vacuum, especially if they trade workplace roles for stay-at-home or work-at-home positions.

When my new world started revolving around nap times and feeding schedules instead of meetings and deadlines, I suffered a loss of respect for myself. Even though caring for children is completely honorable, I still had a nagging feeling that I wasn't contributing to my family or society if I wasn't contributing to my family's bank account. Those little voices of self-doubt are rarely correct, but they are persistent. I found myself searching for something else to fill the gap, so I could feel relevant again.

After my second child was born, I had bouts of tearful frustration when I grew tired of consistently coming in last on the list of household priorities. The baby and the toddler were constantly jockeying for first place. Because my husband was the sole breadwinner and working from home, we prioritized his need for mental and physical space above mine. In our four-person team, the role of mom was an important one yet also the easiest for me—and others—to shortchange.

Like many moms from Detroit to Delhi, I ate after the kids were fed and did chores as the family slept. I was the last to get bathroom time in our one-shower home. Even when it was my turn, I rarely achieved my desired level of privacy. No one dictated these gender norms to me, but it just seemed "natural" to care for myself last.

I know my difficulties are not unique. A 2012 University of Oslo study of over 67,000 mothers of young children found that raising kids had a negative effect on life and marital satisfaction. Participants were asked how satisfied they were in life during stages of pregnancy and postpartum life. Life satisfaction was okay six months after childbirth but took a significant downturn three years later.[10] An earlier study from the University of Nebraska College of Nursing showed that marital happiness scores of subjects who had five- or twenty-four-month-old children were lower than those of childless couples.[11]

What the studies don't measure is *why* life satisfaction is likely to take a downward tumble. I'm not a psychologist, but I believe that—in addition to the lack of sleep—my dip in happiness had everything to do with feeling out of control and disconnected from the person I had spent years becoming. I was holding onto an outdated version of myself, but not living up to it. I needed an updated image combining the new "maternal me" with some kind of higher purpose.

---

[10] "With Kids in the House, Mothers Are Less Satisfied," ScienceNorway.no, February 3, 2012.

[11] P. L. Dalgas-Pelish, "The Impact of the First Child on Marital Happiness," *Journal of Advanced Nursing* 18, no. 3 (March 1993): 437–41.

Story time!

The first time I volunteered with professional people after leaving my job to care for my baby was a little demoralizing because I hadn't yet found a healthy way to define myself.

The meeting took place in a law firm boardroom where the Greater Chicago Food Depository was planning our upcoming gala. As volunteer committee members—women I would have once considered peers—introduced themselves and described their job titles, I felt my sense of self-worth shrinking. What was I now? "Stay-at-home mom?" "Unemployed?"

My insecurities flared when people handed out business cards and I had nothing to offer in return. I worried that my lack of employment would lead to a lack of respect.

CYNTHIA CHANGYIT LEVIN
Mom-at-large

Cindy@myemail.com
(555) 555-5555   妈爱

My early "mommy" business card looked a bit like this image with the Chinese characters for "mother" and "love."

Fortunately, I quickly figured out I could inexpensively print my own business cards at home to bring to the next meeting. The line beneath my name read "Mom-at-Large." It was vague enough to be true and unique enough to prompt a smile from all who read it. It was an early step in redefining myself.

I didn't realize at the time how important these little cards would be when I started visiting congressional offices. The very first thing an aide will do while everyone takes a seat is to pass out cards and ask for yours. My cards gave me a little boost of belonging when I felt like a fish out of water. Plus, they made it a breeze to connect with new moms I met in the neighborhood park!

Who Are You Now?

Your role as mommy will change as your children gain more skills over the years, and it's likely that how you see yourself will evolve as well. You can reinvent yourself as many times as you want—whenever you feel you're due for an upgrade! As an unemployed mother, I had to learn that my self-worth should not rely solely on a job title or paycheck.

There are far more profound ways of measuring yourself, so you can move forward building on your strengths. Empathy, compassion, resourcefulness, humility, and persistence are just a few examples of qualities you can carry with you into your next chapter, which will mean far more than a job title.

Today, I think about how different I was at age twenty-five than at age fifteen. My life changed as I gained more education and moved out on my own. Of course, I would see myself differently! Why, then, did I struggle to keep the same definition of myself in the next ten-year jump when I'd added my husband and children to my life and subtracted a job? I had to learn to recognize the value of my love for my family and to truly believe that all my experiences would serve me well in new ventures.

I invite you to honestly take stock of the person you are now. It will be immensely useful as you think about the kind of advocate, the kind of mom, and the kind of person you want to be.

Story time!

Dr. Radhika Jaladi of Creve Coeur, Missouri didn't need to completely redefine herself as an advocate. But advocacy helped her more fully inhabit the role she had already chosen long ago. She was quite satisfied with her home and work identities. At home, she was "Mom" to two active middle-school boys. At the hospital, she was "Dr. Jaladi" who helped people feel better every day.

When her oldest son began volunteering as an anti-poverty advocate with RESULTS, she attended meetings along with him. Learning more about global health and talking to her members of Congress about it helped her lean even deeper into her identity as a healer.

"As a doctor, I help only the people I come in direct contact with," Radhika says. "However, with advocacy, I can help millions across the world. People I don't know enjoy better health, better opportunities, and a better life."

Who Will You Become?

No matter what kind of mom you are at this moment, you are welcome to join a sisterhood of mothers who found their own personal power by becoming advocates. Nothing makes me feel prouder of who I am than when I consider my part in actually changing the course of human history.

I first started thinking of my accomplishments with pride after I talked to a reporter from a local online news site, the *Morton Grove Patch*. I described a trip to Washington, D.C., where I had talked with lawmakers about vaccines. I thought my interview responses were sort of ho-hum, but the writer described my efforts this way:

> Through the use of social media and face-to-face interactions with local politicians, people like Levin have helped to nearly eradicate diseases such as polio and measles across the globe.

Yes! That's right! I can count myself among the hundreds of thousands of people who have claimed victory over the scourge of polio in almost every country in the world. I began to see myself as a *world changer*!

What words would you use to describe the person *you* want to become? Why not start using them now? They can be serious or silly, as long as they are aspirational to help you get where you want to be. I asked some mom-advocates to list their favorite ways to describe themselves. Their answers are in the picture on the next page. Try some of them on for size!

A change in "job title" can boost your attitude, as I discovered when I created my own business cards. I much prefer to identify myself rather than allow other people to tag me with generic "volunteer" or "stay-at-home mom" labels. It makes all the difference in how I see myself.

A name can also unite a group of activists with a sense of culture and purpose. Activists from Indigenous nations around the world who traveled to Standing Rock Indian Reservation

Image generated from www.wordart.com.

to protest the Dakota Access Pipeline in 2016 united under the name "Water Protectors." The title evokes a cultural, sacred calling to safeguard the land and water and to defend Indigenous people's rights.

In Phoenix, Arizona, Columba Sainz—a climate activist featured earlier in this book—organizes a group of Latina women who call themselves "Ecomadres." She describes her group as "moms that get together in the cafecitos (coffee-shop advocacy gatherings) and learn how environmental issues are affecting our children, then go to our elected officials and tell them how the climate affects our family."

These days, I view myself as an agent of change. That might not be how you would describe me if you saw me typing on my laptop in a cafe or taking a call in my pajamas at home. You might not think it if you saw me walking down a Senate building corridor in my conservative and increasingly matronly outfits with comfortable shoes. But in my mind's eye, I am strong and agile, wearing a black, body-hugging uniform and a vest with many pockets like Marvel's Black Widow. I shape the world around me—not as a dictator, but as part of a team working together to protect humanity. It really doesn't matter if you look heroic. It only matters that you feel it.

Whether you put the words on a homemade business card, type them in an email signature, or just treasure them in your own heart, identify yourself in a way that inspires you to be a little more than you were yesterday.

Story time!

Maxine Thomas of Indianapolis, Indiana, signs emails as "Community Maven," a fun, well-deserved descriptor for a local expert. In addition to caring for her five kids, she looks out for the needs of her neighbors. When the only grocery store in her area suddenly closed, creating a food desert, it was Maxine who organized rides so folks without cars could shop for food.

She loves to serve in her church's soup kitchen because it fills her with a sense of humbleness and grace. Maxine has a totally different attitude, however, when she visits congressional offices in Washington, D.C., to advocate for her community.

"I really feel like I put on a superhero cape because most people don't think what we do is even possible. The work that we do makes our world different, so it sets me in a mood of being extremely powerful. I have the joy of doing something not too many people are doing. I'm excited to come back home and share what I've learned to help others do it, too."

2. Engage Your Brain

I can't overemphasize how important it is to stimulate your intellect during the baby and infant stages of parenting. But sometimes it can feel difficult to remain engaged with the outside world when your life revolves around tiny humans with many needs and few skills.

So many of the tasks you do during these stages are repetitive and require no special talents or creative genius. Babies fill diapers, you change them. Babies get hungry, you feed them. The mechanics of raising a child are quite regular and ordinary. Of course, the skillful, artful part of parenting is performing these acts with love and patience and composure.

It might not seem obvious, but the tedious pace of baby care can actually provide opportunities to intentionally flex and stretch your mind. Use nap time, library time, or tummy time to listen to news, read books, or talk to other parents about the causes you're concerned about. Then, you can be reflective about the knowledge you're absorbing when your sole purpose is to sit still and rock a sleepy baby.

As you start advocating, you will gain chances to meet new people and learn new skills such as writing letters, making phone calls, or organizing fundraisers. Those new skills and new acquaintances may also provide unexpected professional benefits.

For me, volunteer advocacy was the beginning of a career change, even though I wasn't looking for one. Even before I was fully ready to re-enter the job market, I discovered that most nonprofit organizations are fond of hiring dedicated, competent volunteers.

Slim nonprofit budgets mean there's little room for hiring error, so a valuable volunteer who shows a personal commitment to the cause is less risky than a stranger. If you can prove your worth to an organization through volunteer work, you may be able to land a paying position even if you don't meet all the organization's typical preferred characteristics.

Volunteering does not guarantee a job offer, but it happened to me. And I personally know at least eight colleagues who found employment at an organization where they volunteered.

⏱ Story 📖 time!

When her youngest child started preschool, RESULTS volunteer Sarah Borgstede was hired as a research assistant with the Washington D.C.-based organization. They trusted her to work remotely from home in Illinois.

She said, "When I was ready to re-enter the workforce, I couldn't imagine a more fulfilling way to apply my new, kid-free time than by dedicating it in the same place I was volunteering. When a part-time position opened, I was so excited to apply. I think I stood out among the candidates because I understood the mission."

In time, Sarah was promoted to full-time Senior Associate of Program Development with RESULTS.

Even if you don't want a job in the nonprofit sector, the confidence and talents you develop through advocacy can make you an attractive candidate in many fields. Advocacy can help you develop skills in public speaking, meeting facilitation, team leadership, writing, event planning, and training. Those skills can complement almost any profession. Details of your experience speaking directly with members of U.S. Congress look great on a résumé and sound impressive in an interview.

3. Choose Your Own Destiny

A lot of distractions in life can keep a mom from finding her true purpose. It's easy to sink our energy into trivial things rather than focusing on something productive for the greater good. In my own life, I saw this play out regularly at the Morton Grove Mom's Night Out. The monthly gathering was supposed to be a relaxing time for neighborhood moms to kick back with friends. Yet somehow it always devolved into heated arguments about which games to play, how to play them, and who would host the following month. There would be loud debates leaving me feeling emotionally drained over things that just didn't matter.

My friend Laura ruefully chuckled with me as we reminisced about those days together. "So much wasted time. We couldn't get anyone to talk about anything important. We used to have to pull teeth, cajole, or wiggle an issue into our gatherings."

I've long since moved away from that little Chicago suburb, but I heard through the grapevine that one of those moms became a village trustee in charge of the Economic Development Commission. Another went on to be president of the school PTO.

We were all talented, intelligent women, so why did we spend so much precious energy arguing over trivial points at that stage of our lives?

For my group of friends, it's almost like we sold ourselves short in early motherhood because society didn't expect us to take on weighty matters and we didn't expect it of ourselves. Eventually, women either grew tired of the mundane disagreements or were invited into local leadership when the kids grew a bit older. We realized we shouldn't be spending our energy on conflict with each other when there were problems to solve in our community and beyond.

If we aren't intentional about how we use our time, life with kids has a tendency to sweep us along some typical paths whether we want to follow them or not. People will want you to be the Room Mom, Girl Scout Cookie Mom, Soccer Mom, and all kinds of Moms in addition to being Mom to your own family. Those roles are great if they serve your bigger purpose! Just don't get so busy serving others' agendas that you forget to feed your soul and choose your own causes.

Peggy Schaeffer, who volunteers for Bread for the World even in retirement, recalls that she had to learn to be purposeful about how she would spend her time back when she was a mom-advocate with wee ones. Peggy thinks it's healthy for us to ask ourselves, "How do we look at the bigger picture? Do we do things just to be doing? Or do we do things for a bigger purpose?"

We don't have to go into stasis while our kids grow up. We can grow, learn, and affect the world around us no matter how old our children are. Too many mothers look back when older kids become more independent and wonder whether they really had to put their lives on hold while the kids did all the growing and learning. Volunteering to help with kids' activities is absolutely a good thing, but don't get so consumed with cutting out paper leaves for the school project that you forget to find outlets that challenge your brain, too (by the way, my paper leaves are beautiful!).

As we hiked side-by-side with signs at the first Women's March in 2016, new activist Susan Furdek told me, "It's like I've been on a hamster wheel all this time. I've been raising my kids and I haven't gotten anywhere. I feel like I want to get involved and start making a difference."

So, what would it look like in a practical sense to stay off Susan's hamster wheel? You don't have to totally abandon volunteering for your kids' activities. But you should be very clear and specific about what you will or won't do when helping out with classrooms and clubs.

For me, I decided that I could commit to organizing snacks for one school party per child each year (Halloween and Valentine's Day), bringing snacks for sports a few days a season, and chaperoning one school field trip for each of my children. Those tasks all have two things in common. First, they were "one and done" jobs. They wrapped up in a single day that I could plan around. Second, they allowed me—a mom of kids with severe food allergies—to make sure that every student with allergies could be safe and included. Limiting my classroom volunteering to specific tasks helped me be enthusiastically involved while still protecting my valuable advocacy time.

As I became more adept at speaking about poverty in front of others, I was able to engage classes and Scouting troops in whatever advocacy campaign I was working on. That was a way I could volunteer, develop my own voice, and teach our next generation to speak out as well.

Being a champion for a cause you believe in will help you avoid regrets about not making a difference now and down the road. And it can even help you prepare for a new, fulfilling role in a post-kid life!

4. Deepen Friendships

Every childless woman knows that a friend who has a baby will suddenly become less interesting because conversations always loop back to the baby. Early in motherhood, I, too, drove away people with kiddie conversations. Ironically, I didn't actually want to talk about children all the time. Even moms can get tired of their own chatter. We just kind of get stuck in a rut because so much mental energy goes into raising little ones.

But when a mom adds a visit to her senator's office to her schedule, she suddenly has something else to talk about! Whenever you are at a park or a playdate, try starting a conversation with the grown-ups around you about a cause you've been pondering. Some of them will likely be very glad you did.

When I became a mom-advocate, I began inviting moms I met at the library or in the park to join me for Saturday morning "playdates with purpose" (you can find a model of what we did in the "Advocacy Made Easy" section of this book). At every meeting, we would focus on a different topic and learn about it before taking some sort of helpful action. None of us were yet devoted to a specific cause, so we always expanded our minds by learning something new. We sampled a lot of issues and talked about them in a friendly environment while a babysitter kept our kids happily playing downstairs.

When you learn about shocking problems and take action together, you create a bond based on positive feelings like admiration and respect. Working together with intention keeps the conversation focused on something beyond how your parenting styles differ. You're much less likely to argue about the "right way" to potty train.

Finding friends to join me deepened some existing friendships in the Chicago suburb where I lived for twelve years. These kinds of advocacy efforts were even more important in helping me meet people of similar values when I moved to the St. Louis area. Shortly after my move, I purposely sought out like-minded anti-poverty groups, and sure enough, I soon found friends who cared about the same issues I did. More efficient than online dating!

When I took a leap and started going to more conferences in Washington, D.C., I made treasured friends with ease. Not since college had I experienced such rich opportunities to meet interesting people who shared my passions and goals. Traveling and taking a break from caretaking routines opened up space for new information and friendships. Some of my closest friends today are people I met at conferences, and I look forward to seeing them every time we can return.

I met my friends Jennifer DeFranco (left) and Myrdin Thompson (right) at a Shot@Life Conference. They already knew each other from Parenting Magazine's Mom Congress conference the year prior.

5. Empower Yourself

I had to develop a lot of self-confidence when I started visiting congressional offices. Until I actually started meeting in-person with members of Congress and their aides, I couldn't believe that little ol' me could have valuable input. Why would they act on anything I had to say? Don't they spend all their time thinking about these issues already? One particular meeting showed me how wrong my assumptions were.

I recall speaking to a smartly dressed aide in Congresswoman Ann Wagner's office near the end of a long day of advocacy on Capitol Hill. He seemed very professional, very informed, and a little bored. I needed this young man with no spouse and no children to encourage my representative to support life-saving immunization programs for children in poverty around the world. What could I tell him that he didn't already know? How could I get him to move my request about vaccines to the top of the Congresswoman's to-do list?

"Measles," I leaned forward to say, "is a disease we can prevent. It's coming back here to the U.S. and most people have no idea how deadly it is." He listened politely as I informed him that measles killed 400 children, under five years old, every day.

"If we don't vaccinate here in the U.S. and everywhere else, we'll never be rid of it. Measles is so contagious that if one person has it, ninety percent of people nearby who are not immune will become infected. The measles virus can also live for up to *two hours* on a surface or in airspace where an infected person coughed or sneezed." He began to look a little uncomfortable.

Since there had just been a measles outbreak in Disneyland, I shared a little thought experiment that I—a former Disney attractions hostess—had devised. "Imagine a kid with measles sneezes while riding Dumbo the Flying Elephant, where two people sit side-by-side for a ninety-second ride. On a busy day at Disney, sixty-eight people would occupy that place while the virus is still living on the seat and the control buttons. If those other riders were not immunized, a whopping sixty-one of them could walk away with measles while patient zero goes on to infect other attractions."

I had the aide's attention now!

"Ew," he said. "That's disgusting and really alarming."

I agreed and presented the letter that the Congresswoman could sign to support funding for global vaccines. The very next day, I discovered that she had signed the letter. I smiled at the thought that my experience as a mom and theme park enthusiast could have some sway over this young professional's view of viruses.

When I began advocating in person—also known as lobbying—I learned that the aides in Washington, D.C. who decide what is or isn't worth a congressperson's time are typically in their twenties or thirties. Many of them are not parents, so they haven't deeply considered issues from the viewpoint of parents or kids. That's why it is so critical for them to hear from someone who spends her life trying to keep little loved ones healthy and safe, especially regarding funding for education, maternal/child health programs, and other topics directly impacting children.

LaShaun Martin agreed with me when she observed, "Moms bring a unique perspective. We can share and allow others to glean from our life experiences." LaShaun is the National Vice President of Mocha Moms and a Shot@Life advocate. "I felt empowered," she said about the first time she went to a meeting in a congressional office with her Maryland advocacy team. "In times past, I thought it was better to stay silent because my opinion wouldn't matter. But sharing space with others who believe in the same work and seeing actual change motivates me."

The empowerment LaShaun felt can be addictive, in a great way. The surge of confidence that comes from regularly discussing ideas with federal decision-makers and improving policies has carried over into every aspect of my life.

⏱ Story 📖 time!

Laura Frisch, Chicago-area volunteer for Moms Demand Action for Gun Sense in America, described how her first lobbying day in the Illinois capital gave her a sense of empowerment.

> We all wore our loveliest Sunday dresses. We were looking for members of Congress to get a yes on a bill. I'm thinking, "I can do this! I'm changing the world and making my kids safer!" During the day, we saw State Representative Daniel Biss, who I knew personally. When we spoke to him, he took us aside and said, "Don't ask me to vote for a bill. Ask me to co-sponsor."
>
> That was a great and humbling experience to have him explain to us that co-sponsorship is a way to get a member on the record, while a verbal "yes" doesn't hold them accountable, especially if the bill never comes to a vote.
>
> The next representative we saw was a guy with a smarmy political attitude saying, "Have a seat, little ladies. What can I do for you? So, what are you asking me to vote for?"

With our newfound advice, we confidently replied, "We're not asking you to vote for anything right now. We want you to be a co-sponsor."

His tone altered from condescending to cautious. That was the moment that we thought, "We have literally changed this game."

Laura had discovered her first taste of power as an insider.

Oddly, the things that make me special on Capitol Hill today are exactly the traits that made me feel inadequate in the beginning. I was an ordinary citizen with no professional expertise. I felt so strongly about my cause that I spent my own personal time and money to travel to Washington, D.C. Most importantly, I was not a paid lobbyist. I thought those things made me a nobody. On the contrary, those are characteristics that make volunteers interesting to many members of Congress. Concerned citizens who go to such lengths to seek out reasonable dialogue are a rare breed.

I am a "constituent," which means I live in the area that my elected officials represent. Additionally, I'm a taxpayer who helps pay their salaries, and an active voter. So, there are three very good reasons my members of Congress should care about my opinion. A person in their district, who makes the effort to have regular personal meetings, can help an elected official do a good job. Yet such engaged constituents can also swiftly turn and organize for an opponent if they don't feel respected. Wise politicians will take care to keep up their end of the relationship.

There are hundreds of urgent issues competing for the attention of any given member of Congress and thousands of important ones sitting on the back burner not addressed at all. I absolutely have important ideas to share about some of those underrepresented topics that never float to the top of the inbox by themselves. We can all move our issues up the stack by persistently contacting the offices of people paid by our own tax dollars. Our members of Congress and their staffers are supposed to work for us.

Of course, once you open the door to thinking of yourself as worthy, you can't close it for the other parts of your life. So, here is fair warning: if you join me on this path, you may find yourself walking taller around the playground and experiencing regular bouts of self-confidence!

It's Your Turn!

1. How would you describe yourself? Write down some words that illustrate the kind of person and mother that you want to be. Can adding advocacy into your life help you become that version of yourself?
2. How are you different than you were before becoming a mother? How are you the same?
3. Do you feel that your job title—or lack of one—defines your identity? Are you content with that definition, or could it use an upgrade?
4. If you are unemployed or have a job that is unsatisfying, could advocacy provide satisfaction that you're helping someone else? If you have a job that you like, how might advocacy enhance that work or provide a different kind of satisfaction?

5. Do you think you currently feel empowered enough to make a request of a senator or congressperson? Why or why not? Would it make a difference if you were asking for something that was not to benefit you personally, but for other people instead?

6. Who in your social circle might have skills or resources that could complement yours to help you with your advocacy ideas? Who might offer some moral support for you trying something new?

Notes

CHAPTER 8

CAN ADVOCACY MAKE YOUR KIDS' LIVES BETTER?

I TOOK MY CHILDREN, ages six and eight, to meet with Congresswoman Jan Schakowsky on a summer afternoon to lobby for global vaccines on behalf of the UN Foundation's Shot@Life campaign. Besides just looking cute, my kids had been assigned the task of showing the congresswoman a newspaper article describing an awareness event we had hosted for moms and kids at our house.

After fulfilling her role, my youngest daughter grew utterly bored with the topic of program funding and started to create a picture of all of us. After our discussion, the congresswoman glanced over at her masterpiece. "Is that me?" she asked, pointing to a figure in the drawing.

"Yes, and that's me and my sister and that's Mommy," my artist proudly proclaimed.

The congresswoman smiled. "You know what? I really like this picture because I'm pretty short and you drew me taller than everyone! I love it!" Congresswoman Schakowsky then leaned in to give a brief and furious tickle to my now-giggling daughter.

Wow, I thought. I would never, ever have imagined having that kind of familiar relationship with someone so important at that age. If my kids aren't afraid of their representative now, what in the world will they accomplish with their members of Congress when they're all grown up?

I still smile when I think of that bond between my kids and my congresswoman, a person I had initially been scared to meet. I had never even seen a U.S. representative in real life before our first meeting, and my sweaty palms and wavering voice put my nervousness on full display back then.

My children will have hurdles to overcome in their lives, but they will never think they aren't worthy to speak with a member of Congress. They might even think it's strange *not* to check in with their elected officials from time to time. Sure, they may not choose to become anti-poverty advocates—or any type of activist at all. But if they discover they cannot stay silent about an issue, my daughters will have the tools they need to speak out. Together, we've already removed the barrier that makes most people wonder, "Can we really talk to Congress? Will it even make a difference?"

I have met mothers who are hesitant to involve their children in advocacy for various reasons. Some tykes simply can't sit still in a meeting. Some moms feel like they can barely get themselves organized to take action, much less include kids and all the accompanying chaos. I admit that it depends on the individual personalities and readiness levels of both parent and child. We each have to measure the pros and cons of nurturing advocacy with our particular children.

Since it's far easier for most of us to rattle off all the cons, let me share some of the less obvious pros. What can your kids gain if you involve them in advocacy activities?

- Confidence and skill to express themselves
- Ability to stick up for themselves and others
- Empathy, compassion, and respect
- Knowledge of how their government works
- Understanding of how inequality and oppression affect our lives

They may also *lose* something: the feeling of being intimidated by people in power. When kids meet members of Congress as they are growing up, the mystique falls away. They—and you—will realize that the people running our government are human, too.

Age-Appropriate Actions to Take with Your Child

Obviously, your kids' ability to join you in advocacy actions will vary depending on their ages, abilities, temperaments, and interests. But here are some activities I've enjoyed with my children that you can undertake with your kids at various ages and stages. I learned and adapted as my children grew.

Tiny Babies

- Attend a meeting in a baby carrier
- Make a handprint to put at the end of a parent's letter using an ink pad

Toddlers

- Draw pictures to send to Congress (you might need to include some captions to interpret the drawings)
- Talk with you about your cause in a video you can share on social media
- Listen as you read picture books about caring, equality, and changing the world

Grade Schoolers

- Write letters to Congress
- Write a statement and read it aloud in a lobby meeting
- Present a cause to a Scouting group
- Make a poster for a member of Congress
- Make a video about an issue

Middle Schoolers

- Write a letter to the editor
- Make a phone call to Congress
- Write an email to Congress
- Speak in a lobby meeting

High Schoolers

↵ Organize a letter-writing or social media action
↵ Write an opinion piece for the editorial page of your newspaper
↵ Lead a lobby meeting
↵ Attend an advocacy conference

There's a lot of flexibility in those lists. Of course, older kids can do activities listed for younger kids. Some adult advocates will never do the activities I listed for high schoolers, while I've known outstanding middle-schoolers who have attended conferences and led lobby meetings. Don't feel pressured to check them all off. Do only what your kids feel comfortable with. It's a menu, not a shopping list!

What Do the Kids Think?

When my kids were in elementary school, they described some of the benefits they reaped from being involved in my advocacy work.

↵ "I get candy at class trivia time because nobody else knows the answers to questions like, 'How many U.S. representatives are in Congress?'"
↵ "Congressman Lacy Clay gives us toys and other prizes when we visit him in his Washington, D.C., office."
↵ "Sometimes Mom takes me out of school to talk to congresspeople."
↵ "People in Washington listen and treat us more like adults than other people at home."

Of course, at the time, their favorite parts involved prizes and skipping school! With my adult eyes, however, I could see they gained much more than that. I can also tell you stories about how my kids used skills they learned from our activities to employ activism in their own lives.

For example, in third grade, after a lesson about the civil disobedience of Rosa Parks, my oldest daughter led a sit-in to protest the unfair treatment of a classmate who had his soccer privileges taken away by a playground supervisor with a history of treating the kids poorly. When challenged, they requested a meeting with the assistant principal of the school. Three students composed a list of legitimate grievances and prepared a summary document for the principal written in blue Crayola marker. The meeting proceeded in a peaceful and professional manner. Soccer privileges were restored. She still vividly remembers this story today.

As teens, their experiences continue to aid them academically. I've lost track of the number of times they were able to use statistics and facts they knew from advocacy work in term papers, speech classes, Model UN events, and even a Latin essay! But perhaps the biggest benefit came to light when our world turned upside-down as COVID-19 cases reached the United States in 2020. We were one of the first families in our community to stop dining indoors at restaurants, attending choir rehearsals, and going to Taekwondo practice. Why? Because in early January, my tenth grader had read about a new virus gaining traction in China and thought, "Is that going to be a problem?"

By March, it was clear we were part of a pandemic story not unlike the stories of polio, tuberculosis, and HIV/AIDS outbreaks that we regularly described to congressional staff. Not once did I need to have a conversation with either of my teenagers to convince them that isolating at home was the wise and kind thing to do for ourselves and our community. There was no whining about wanting to go see friends because "everyone else was doing it." They knew all too well how viruses spread and what was at stake.

By April, my sophomore had two opinion pieces about COVID-19 and the importance of U.S. foreign assistance published in global health publications. Her media advocacy pieces were a tremendous outlet for her anxieties about the coronavirus, a boost to her confidence, an education for all who read them, and respectable additions to her college application portfolio.

Setting a Mighty Example

My mom used to describe her kids as "little pitchers with big ears." Our big ears were listening to everything she was saying, even when we didn't realize we were paying attention. Your kids are listening to you, too. What are you pouring into your little pitchers?

What will your kids think you care most about: the petty slights of annoying people or whether every student in your city has access to quality education? Do they hear more about what material things you want for yourself or about your desire to help everyone in your community have things they need?

Like it or not, your children are constantly observing and learning from you. Mine see plenty of my nail-biting, junk-food-eating, bad habits despite my efforts not to pass those along. I owe it to them, to myself, and to the world to also provide tangible examples of how I can make a positive impact in our lives.

Story time!

Cathy Lyons-Spear discovered that her daughter was watching her example even when adults thought their kids were focused on playtime. Cathy has been a RESULTS volunteer in Asheville, North Carolina for over twenty-five years. Early in her advocacy, she became the group leader for her local RESULTS chapter, hosting monthly meetings to discuss and take action on child survival issues.

"When I started, most of the time the two youngest ones would end up sort of playing with Barbie dolls or something in the room we were meeting in," Cathy said. "So, they got a lot of stuff just from listening and processing it in their heads. One day when my daughter was in second grade, they were studying jobs and occupations in school. They went around the room to say what their parents did as an occupation. Lindsay said, 'Well, my dad builds houses . . . but my mom saves the world.'"

What a testimony of how Cathy's daughter viewed her mother's volunteer work—and her mother!

We all want our children to see the best sides of ourselves. To do that, we first have to recognize the best that is within ourselves. Then we can wear it on the outside for everyone—including our kids—to behold.

My children have had ringside seats to watch their mother speak out against hunger, disease, and gender inequality for as long as they can remember. When big historic moments happen, I do think about what I want them to remember from those days. What did we do when children of immigrants and refugees were separated from their families and detained at our border in cages? What memories will they have about the year when thousands of protestors lined the streets opposing systemic racism toward Black Americans? They won't have to ask me what I was doing because they were always beside me watching and listening.

To be sure, they also still hear me complain some days about the guy who took my parking space. I'm only human. Yet I am optimistic that my selfish slip-ups will be balanced out by the hours we spend together saving the world.

It's Your Turn!

1. What has your child heard you complain about in the last twenty-four hours? Were they things that really matter or superficial irritations? (If you don't know, ask your kid.)
2. Listen to the discussions of other parents in your peer group. Are you surrounding yourself with people who are full of complaints but no solutions?
3. Do you belong to community groups or online communities that provide positive dialogue and encourage constructive thoughts and actions? Where could you look for friends or groups that will help fill you up with inspiration and foster constructive behavior?
4. Do your kids seem aware of people who are struggling? Are they sympathetic? How can you help them nurture empathy?
5. Have your kids ever seen you take action for a cause you believe in? If so, what was it?
6. How would your children describe what you do during the day? Have you given them opportunities or reasons to see you as someone who "saves the world?"

Elena Hung

Photo provided by Elena Hung.

CHAPTER 9

PROFILE: ELENA HUNG
TELLING STORIES TO POWER

AS THE EXECUTIVE DIRECTOR and co-founder of Little Lobbyists, Elena Hung advocates to protect and expand the rights of children who have complex medical needs and disabilities. Elena's advocacy grows from her role as the fiercely loving mother of Xiomara.

When I interviewed her mom, Xiomara was a spunky first grader who loved playing with her big brother, watching *Sesame Street*, and going to the library. She had spent her entire life battling several serious medical conditions affecting her airways, lungs, heart, and kidneys. She experienced tracheobronchomalacia, which means her airway and lungs were floppy and collapsed when she breathed. She relied on an ever-present tracheostomy tube to deliver air to her lungs and a feeding tube to deliver all her nutrition.

Elena didn't set out to become an activist and certainly didn't intend to start an organization, but in 2017, she watched with fear as Congress attempted to repeal the Affordable Care Act (ACA). She believed their actions would endanger her daughter, as ten pre-existing conditions would make it hard to receive medical insurance, without the ACA's protection for people with such conditions.

In a moment of hope and desperation, Elena thought, "We have to do something. Just show up." She knew senators would never fight for anyone like Xiomara if they had never met anyone like her.

Elena lived in Maryland, close to Washington, D.C., and she was also part of a nationwide community of families with children like hers. Most of those families lived too far away to access offices of U.S. senators.

In a late-night discussion, Elena and her mom-friend Michelle Morrison formed a basic plan. The parents who lived near D.C. would visit legislators in support of the ACA, sharing pictures and stories of kids with complex medical needs who lived all over the country. When they delivered their message, they would bring along their own kids, so everyone in a senator's office could personally meet disabled children with trach tubes, ventilators, oxygen, wheelchairs, walkers, and feeding tubes. They wanted lawmakers to come face-to-face with children who desperately needed the continued protection of the ACA and access to Medicaid and hear stories about other kids in similar situations all over the country.

Elena and the other parents planned their efforts carefully and intentionally, but they had no idea how they would be received. Members of Congress were generally surprised by the presence of these tiny visitors and all their accompanying medical equipment. Elena explained, "Children are not your usual visitors on Capitol

Hill. It's historically filled with lobbyists; powerful men in suits and powerful women in suits and high heels. The first reaction is usually, 'Oh! What are you doing here? Are you lost?' I don't mean that in a positive or negative way. It's just something they're not used to. The more often we go, the more welcoming it is among the members who have gotten to know us."

In a dramatic vote a month after those visits, the Senate voted down the ACA repeal, protecting Xiomara's health insurance and access to Medicaid—for the moment, at least.

It was obvious to Elena that more work was needed, so she and Michelle continued to collect and deliver stories from parents. They visited Capitol Hill repeatedly with their kids and became friendly with influential politicians like Nancy Pelosi and Elizabeth Warren. The more often they visited, Elena discovered, the more they were welcomed by members who grew to know them. In 2018, Little Lobbyists became an official nonprofit 501(c)(4) lobbying organization.

The nature of the visits changed a lot in the years after the summer of 2017. Those first meetings were very urgent, Elena recalled. "It was like, 'You have to vote this way *now!*' There wasn't a whole lot of room or space to develop a relationship."

Over the next few years, the Little Lobbyist families realized that building relationships can be an important step toward impactful change. The families concentrated on telling powerful stories about their kids' lives, getting to know aides and members of Congress, and learning how to work together with legislators instead of focusing on a certain vote.

Elena wants members of Congress and their staff to understand these children with complex medical needs and disabilities and to recognize how those needs impact families. She also wants legislators to call on her as a resource if they face questions about such issues. "I have this wealth of knowledge and personal experience that you cannot get from policy experts or data analysts."

Even though Elena has a background as an attorney, she doesn't speak in complicated legalese when she wants to make a point. Instead, she uses her sincere mom voice to describe her family life and share her hopes and fears for her child's future. As Xiomara's mother, she offers a valuable perspective no one else can provide, and she considers a continuing conversation a kind of victory.

When a legislator ends a discussion by suggesting a future meeting, Elena feels very satisfied. "That feels hopeful like we are working together toward something larger that is sustainable and working toward more permanent change."

PART II

HOW TO GET STARTED

NOW THAT I HAVE introduced you to advocacy and convinced you that moms make great advocates, I'm tempted to hand you a list of great advocacy organizations and let you go at it! But you might not be quite ready for that step yet (if you are, feel free to skip to Part III, pick out an action, and dive right in).

Perhaps you accept that *some* moms make great advocates but still aren't sure how to make it work in your own busy life. Maybe you're worried you'll make a mistake or get laughed at. Maybe you are passionate about many causes and don't know which one to address first.

Don't be discouraged if you're feeling overwhelmed and aren't sure where to begin. That's exactly how I began my advocacy. I was lucky to find great mentors to help me get started, and I want to help you as they helped me. My first piece of advice may sound simplistic, but it is effective: **Begin where you are.**

Being a bookish sort of girl, I began by reading. I read books about poverty and books about solutions. I gave myself time to read and digest the information emotionally. Reading was a great place for me to start because that is where I was already, both literally and metaphorically. I spent a lot of time rocking a baby every day, which gave me many opportunities to pick up a book like *The End of Poverty* by Jeffrey Sachs in between *Game of Thrones* novels.

I was also at a time in my life when reading was just about the only activity I was sure I could handle. I wanted to help mothers in poverty, but I was woefully uninformed about the state of impoverished women and children in the world and clueless about how to help. I didn't come out of a family tradition of activism, so I didn't even know that writing a letter to Congress was a useful thing to do.

"Advocacy" wasn't in my active vocabulary. Nursing a baby every few hours left me feeling disheveled and ragged, and I had little motivation to get out in public. But I had a desire to help and time to read.

Only later, when I was spending most of my days shuttling daughters between sports and music lessons, could I appreciate what a blessed combination that had been: "A desire to help and time to read." Back then, I was feeling lonely and isolated. Now, I realize that I was one of the luckiest and most privileged women on the face of the earth. How many women without access to electricity, healthcare, or food would love to be able to indulge a desire to help and time to read?

Maybe you are at that stage right now yourself. You want to help but don't know how to start. Well, hang on to that desire and keep reading.

Notes

CHAPTER 10

WHERE DO I START?

WHEN I WAS A long-distance runner, I was inspired by a quote from Chinese philosopher Lao-Tzu. It's commonly rendered as "The journey of a thousand miles begins with a single step," which makes it great advice for runners beginning marathon training or for an activist about to start a new project.

However, I learned this proverb can also be translated as "The journey of a thousand miles begins *beneath one's feet.*" This version could provide the perfect starting point for a mom who wants to become an advocate. Instead of emphasizing the action of the first step, this version of the proverb advises a would-be traveler to start from a place of stillness.

Stillness doesn't necessarily mean inactivity. In our stillness, we can reflect upon our lives and dreams. During emotional turmoil (sorrow over dying children, doubts about your own abilities, lack of sleep from baby care), take a moment to ponder the following questions:

- ↵ Where are you standing in your life right now—as a person and as a parent?
- ↵ What aspect of our broken world do you want to help fix?
- ↵ What skills can you bring to the party at this moment?
- ↵ What skills would you like to develop?

Depending on your answers, you could end up choosing a very different path than the one you're used to taking. Before I started my advocacy efforts, I would have inadvertently responded to the "Where are you now?" question by answering a different question: "Where were you before?" I was so used to seeing myself as a corporate employee that I was incapable of seeing myself as anything else. I could have saved myself a lot of soul searching by recognizing that I was "a really tired mom of two, trying to figure out how to get through the day, with this super-annoying eye twitch caused by sleep deprivation and child-induced stress."

You don't have to have all the answers right away. Intentionally pausing for inner reflection will ground you and help you see what is beneath your feet before you make a first move. Hiking survival teachers advise us to be still and look at our surroundings for clues about our location when we are lost. You must determine where you are before you can figure out how to get where you want to be.

Three Roads to Advocacy

If you want to become a world changer, there are three main paths you could follow. Each has advantages and disadvantages, depending on your personality and what resources are available to you. Think about where you are now, consider where you want to be, and determine which of these paths is most likely to get you there with the fewest detours.

1. Begin with Others

Advantage. Friends and colleagues provide support and keep you accountable. You can learn together. Making a commitment to others provides an incredible incentive to stick to a plan and make progress toward your goals. Joining a reputable advocacy group filled with supportive people can provide a structure to get involved and stay involved. A successful, committed group also allows you to quickly see that your actions have a big impact!

Disadvantage. It can be challenging to rally others if you don't have a group of willing friends or an advocacy group in your neighborhood already (I didn't). This gets easier when you have more practice, but it is especially difficult to recruit and lead a group of beginners before you learn some basic advocacy skills.

2. Begin by Yourself

Advantage. This path often looks very appealing for the introspective, self-motivated type, because you can move at your own pace. You don't have to worry about others witnessing your learning curve, and you won't have to make any compromises on scheduling or communication styles that are out of your comfort zone.

Disadvantage. It's extremely hard to keep up a sense of urgency when you have no teammates or mentors. You don't get to learn from others or be encouraged by them.

3. Begin with Kids

Advantage. You get to see the minds of your children expand before your eyes, which is incredibly inspirational. If you are a teacher or Scout troop leader, you already have little teammates to help out and those efforts can also help you fulfill your leadership obligations as well. Multitasking win!

Disadvantage. It's wise to have your act together before you open your mouth with kids. I swear they can smell uncertainty and ask all sorts of questions to expose it! My own children do benefit from watching me figure things out at home, but I highly recommend getting organized before presenting in front of a group of squirrely grade-schoolers.

 Story time!

Bernadette O'Neil is a St. Louis mom-activist who chose to start her advocacy with others. She prefers rallies and protests to one-on-one actions. For Bernadette, making a phone call to Congress by herself was harder for her than going to a political rally. "There's a whole lot of conditioning to sit down and shut up that kicks in when I'm alone," she explained. But in crowds, she felt stronger.

With the support of a committed RESULTS group, which included other mothers, Bernadette learned how to speak face-to-face with her U.S. representative and tell powerful stories with confidence. Still, she found beginning with gatherings of activists was a powerful antidote to solitary, negative thoughts of self-doubt.

Where Can I Make the Most Difference?

You will make the most difference on an issue that you are personally passionate about. The choice of where to engage is obvious to some, but not all. Mothers facing situations that immediately threaten their children usually see their missions with clarity. For example, families who can't afford critical medical treatment or who are threatened by unsafe living conditions need to advocate for their very survival. Mothers who have lost a loved one in a shooting might want to take action against gun violence. Ultimately, this is something each person has to answer individually.

For me, I was sure that I wanted to start fighting for mothers and babies in poverty because I had become increasingly aware of my privilege and felt a need to help mothers who did not have those same resources. If an issue or a situation is keeping you up at night, lean into that feeling. Being part of the solution might be what you need to ease your anxiety.

Children are going to bed with hungry bellies. Oceans are polluted. Girls in poverty need access to education. Preventable diseases cause millions of unnecessary deaths each year. Neurodiverse children need accommodations at school. Racial oppression and white supremacy affect all sorts of issues, including healthcare inequality and mass incarceration. Our world is broken in so many ways that you don't have to look very hard to find a cause to support. Believe me, there is a problem crying out for your attention. It's up to you to listen when your own heart starts telling you to "do something!"

Cara Fleischer chose to fight for an issue that threatened her own family. Her climate activism took root in the frightening days when her infant daughter was gasping for breath due to asthma she developed in the smoggy air of Atlanta, GA. Cara moved back to her home state of Florida seeking cleaner air but discovered that climate change had caused storms to be more intense and frequent. After a summer when four hurricanes and smoke from forestry and waste burns threatened her family—which had expanded to include a baby boy—Cara realized she needed to become active in changing environmental policy for the safety of her children and others.

"The knowledge that the environment was hurting my children's health was eating away at me, but I felt overwhelmed," Cara said. "I was a happy, peaceful person by nature who didn't go out seeking fights or soapboxes. Where did I fit into all this? One clear and wide-eyed day, I realized that this was my defining purpose, the one issue that kept me up at night, and if I wasn't willing to try to make a difference now when my family was on the line, then when?"

Build Your Skills

Whether or not you've found an issue that you are sure is your personal calling, I highly recommend you look for an organization with a mission you fundamentally agree with and a dedication to empowering volunteers. Find a group that will support and take care of you. Regular meetings and individual coaching for volunteers are hallmarks of groups that take volunteer development seriously. If you join a group that is as excited about developing your individual voice as advancing its cause, you will develop great skills to tackle any issue that grabs your heart in the future!

Find Your Cause

You may be feeling dissatisfied about the state of the world in general and don't yet see how you can focus on just one issue. The question of where to put your efforts is the magic question that no one can answer for you, but here are a few ways to jump-start your thinking.

- **Read** *The Path: Creating Your Mission Statement for Work and for Life* by Laurie Beth Jones and answer the questions in it thoughtfully and truthfully. I read the book about a year before I became pregnant when I was questioning whether I wanted to stay in my career as an engineer. I wrote my answers down on a paper and tucked them in the book. Years later, when I was an accomplished advocate, I revisited my list when it randomly fell out of the book and realized how pivotal that exercise had been in finding a direction for myself.

- **Get Informed.** For me, listening to NPR on my bedroom radio was an important part of broadening my awareness of global problems. Reading your local paper or a paper that covers global issues like the Washington Post or the New York Times can do the same thing, although I admit it was easier to multi-task with the radio than a newspaper. If you attend a house of worship, sometimes they will have programs with childcare where you can find out about social issues the congregation cares about.

- **Fill a need.** Sam Daley-Harris, the founder of RESULTS, is fond of repeating this Buckminster Fuller quote in his distinctive, deliberate style: "The things to do are: the things that need doing, that you see need to be done, and that no one else seems to see need to be done." Go ahead and read that again. It was a little complicated for me the first time I heard it, too!

The entire quote goes on to say, "Then you will conceive your own way of doing that which needs to be done—that no one else has told you to do or how to do it. This will bring out the real you that often gets buried inside a character that has acquired a superficial array of behaviors induced or imposed by others on the individual." Basically, pick an issue that you believe is neglected by others and work on it in your own special way!

◁ **Save some lives.** This advice is open to your interpretation. You can decide whether you want to think of it literally or figuratively and whether you want to save the lives of humans, dogs, whales, or any of the many living things in our planet's fragile ecosystem. An everyday citizen who learns the skills to advocate to our elected officials is democracy at its finest. To save lives with those skills is humanity at its finest.

Find Your Focus

One of the most useful pieces of advice I ever got was from another activist over lunch during my early days of advocacy, when I was full of energy but very little strategy. Over a plate of noodles, I bombarded her with all my hopes, passions, charity collection projects, and committees. My interests ranged from local food pantries to global starvation, from microcredit lending to global warming, from child mortality to U.S. education. She patiently listened to my effusive outpouring and then gently suggested that I might want to focus a bit. She was—quite rightly—advising that I might be far more effective if I focused on one thing.

I am happy to offer that advice to you today, even though I still struggle to take the advice I so freely dispense. Today, I can say I am mainly a global poverty activist, but my focus is still quite broad. Bouncing between the issues of global education and global health is easy because the topics are closely related and because I was lucky enough to find an organization, RESULTS, that sees the connection between those issues. Volunteering with them allows me to work on both of those as well as on several aspects of U.S. poverty. I do still lend my voice to select other causes I care about. However, developing a specialty in global health has put me in a position to have far greater impact than when I was more scattered.

Pick an Action that Fits Your Current Schedule

Whether you are working in or out of the home, having kids of any age means you have limited time to volunteer. Not to worry! Becoming a world changer does not always actually require oodles of time, as you can see from these suggestions.

What Can You Do in the Middle of the Night?

- Read something inspirational on your favorite issue
- Browse the internet for other organizations and individuals doing the kind of work that interests you
- Leave a voicemail for a congressional office
- Post an interesting article on social media so your friends will find it in the morning
- Plan how to talk to kids or other parents about your issue to build awareness or recruit other helpers
- Write a blog post

- Sign an online petition
- Write a letter to the editor

Got Two Minutes?

- Take an online advocacy action (Twitter, Facebook)
- Leave a message for a member of Congress

Got Ten Minutes?

- Handwrite a few letters to your members of Congress. Work from a sample letter from a trusted advocacy organization. After you write the first one to your representative, it will only take about three minutes to copy the same message for each of your senators.
- Post on social media encouraging your friends to take an advocacy action

Got More Time?

- Reach out to organizations working on your issues and set up a coffee date with local activists. I've provided a list of some excellent organizations in the appendices.
- Call your kids' teachers or Scout leader to ask if you can talk to their students about your issue
- Do some relationship building with the aides in your congressional offices: call them to introduce yourself, follow up on an earlier action, say thank you for something your member of

Congress has done, or make an appointment to meet them in their local office.

◁ Arrange a letter-writing meeting so your friends can learn about your issue and write to Congress with you

◁ Write several letters to the editors of multiple newspapers

Take a Big Leap: Attend an Advocacy Conference

If you take my advice and get involved with a reputable national advocacy organization, you will likely have an opportunity to participate in a conference with a "Lobby Day" that offers a chance to meet members of Congress in Washington, D.C., or in your state capital. "Lobbying" refers to meeting with a member of Congress for the purpose of persuading them to support your cause. Sessions with experts and inspirational speakers prepare volunteers for face-to-face meetings with lawmakers and their aides.

I especially suggest that new advocates go to an advocacy conference so they can quickly get up to speed and network with other volunteers. You can share ideas and work together even after the event. Time away from your kids is precious and rare. Make the most of it by choosing a conference run by an organization dedicated to truly empowering its volunteers and developing the voices of its members. Those groups invest in sessions to teach a variety of organizing and advocacy techniques, so you can return home with valuable allies and tools to help you beyond Lobby Day.

The best organizations will stay in touch with you when you return home. Having strong post-conference support reduces the likelihood of activists quitting out of frustration or drifting away as we head back into everyday habits and routines.

I still go to conferences to hear the latest updates on my issues and to lobby in force on Capitol Hill with hundreds of other volunteers. Plus, the advocates I've met along the way have become some of my best friends, so it's a reunion party every time we get together. Their friendship and support keep me engaged and excited about the work we do all year, year after year.

 Tips and Ideas

Tips to network with diverse allies at a conference

Let's face it, most big world problems are caused or worsened by inequality. To combat that, diverse allies need to work together. I find everyday social circles tend to foster interactions with people of similar income level, ethnicity, age, and educational experience. Building relationships at anti-poverty events with people from other countries and communities widens my worldview. Diversity in advocacy friendships discourages stereotyping and can help dismantle oppressive systems shaped by racism, classism, ableism, ageism, homophobia, and more.

- Choose conference sessions on topics that will challenge your usual patterns of thinking.
- Purposefully mingle with advocates who are different from you in some way.
- Find ways to actively work with new colleagues after the conference. Guest blogging, brainstorming advocacy ideas, or simply encouraging each other on social media can keep you in touch until the next gathering.

It's Your Turn!

1. Assess your personality and your life situation to help you choose how to start advocating. Do you tend to be introverted or extroverted? Are you easily self-motivated or someone who needs a nudge to get things done? Do you have people to support you or would you like to seek out some advocacy partners?

2. Would you like to take action with your kids? Are you spending a lot of time alone while your baby naps? How can these factors influence where you begin your advocacy adventure?

3. Do you feel called to work on a certain issue or toward a particular goal? Are there local or national organizations working on this need that could use your help doing the work in your own community? Will joining them provide personal support to get you started?

4. What is the most important thing you wish you could change for the better in the world your children will live in?

5. Do you have resources to get to a national conference? Can you brainstorm about people who might help watch your kids while you are away or faith groups who might help pay for your travel? Are there scholarships offered by conferences that can help with expenses?

Teresa Rugg

Photo credit: Amber Strehle.

CHAPTER 11

PROFILE: TERESA RUGG ADVOCATING YOUR OWN WAY

TERESA RUGG GETS A job done, even though she doesn't always do it the conventional way. I admire her ability to walk the delicate line of working within systems while reframing the norms around her. She doesn't break rules—not usually anyway—but she definitely tests their flexibility. I think of her as highly skilled at "bending the curve."

Teresa once took me on a run in her little town of Snohomish, Washington, while describing a bit about her local advocacy. An avid runner, Teresa noticed a hazardous corner on her daily route. Although it wasn't a terribly busy intersection, the rural environment made it more dangerous because drivers were not used to seeing people in the bike lane when they made a right turn.

Teresa recognized that drivers would have a better chance of seeing pedestrians or cyclists if the shoulder lines on the right side of the road were bent away from the curb just a bit more. She persistently voiced her concern to county officials with repeated emails and phone calls, finally convincing them to make her suggested change in the road. That small improvement probably prevented a terrible tragedy.

Teresa Rugg standing beside the road lines that were changed because of her activism.

Teresa saw something that needed to be changed and spoke out for her own safety and that of her neighbors. The solution didn't cost much money, but it has a daily impact.

But that is not the only curve Teresa has been bending.

Teresa joined RESULTS in 2004 when she wrote her first letter to a member of Congress. She had attended a meeting where she learned to write short, powerful letters about child survival. Thanks to the work of activists before her, U.S. support for the issue had been rising since the 1980s when a revolution in child survival began around the world. For instance, the United States Agency for International Development (USAID) funding for global child survival and maternal health programs had risen from $132.2 million per year in 1985 to $442.9 million in 2004.[12]

Consequently, the number of global child deaths was consistently falling. By the time Teresa wrote her letter, it was no longer normal to lose 14.5 million infants and children per year (around 40,000 kids under-five deaths per day!) as we did in the mid-1980's.[13] And by 2019, UNICEF, the World Health Organization, and the World Bank all reported that an average of only 5.2 million children under five were dying each year. That is tremendous progress, but 14,000 little ones dying each day is still far too many. Plus, experts fear that the COVID-19 pandemic may set us back by ten to twenty years or more because of factors like disruptions to routine vaccines, nutrition, and family income. So advocates must continue to fight to bend the deadly data curve further downward every single year—until it hits zero.[14]

Back in 2004, Teresa felt pretty good about the letter she wrote for RESULTS but didn't think much more about it as she returned to chasing her two- and four-year-old kids. Then an aide from U.S. Representative Rick Larson's D.C. office called about her compelling letter. He assured Teresa that her congressman had read the letter personally and would indeed co-sponsor the bill she had brought to his attention.

---

[12] USAID report, "Two Decades of Progress: USAID'S Child Survival and Maternal Health Program," June 2009.

[13] UNICEF report, "The State of the World's Children 1987," Author: James P. Grant.

[14] UNICEF report, "Levels & Trends in Child Mortality, Report 2020, Estimates developed by the UN Inter-agency Group for Child Mortality Estimation"; and World Health Organization, "COVID-19 Could Reverse Decades of Progress Toward Eliminating Preventable Child Deaths, Agencies Warn," Sept. 9, 2020.

Number of Under-Five Deaths

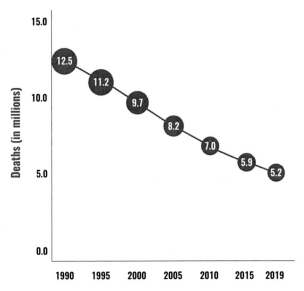

* Data from UNICEF-2020-Child-Mortality-Report.pdf "Levels & Trends in Child Mortality, Report 2020, Estimates developed by the UN Inter-agency Group for Child Mortality Estimation"

Teresa was elated with her ability to influence a decision-maker so quickly. "I was hooked for life!" She was not at her best when she picked up that call from her congressman's office. She recalled, "I was sick and had a horrible voice. No mute button, children climbing up my leg, and laryngitis. I wanted to scream with excitement afterwards, but I couldn't!" She had just received living proof that one person speaking out can really make a difference—even without an actual voice.

Teresa definitely wanted to continue, but the structure of RESULTS meetings made it tough for a mom of preschoolers to be involved. Back then, as now, the organization was known for consistently training volunteers to be effective lobbyists using highly successful techniques. But it also relied on rigorous standards for integrating new members and holding group meetings.

In an era before digital webinars and video conferencing were commonplace, such tactics were a vital component of building a cohesive organization. In-person meetings where members could practice speeches live were critical for the quality of training nationwide.

Yet the rigid nature of the group culture could be limiting. Meetings held on Saturday afternoons—prime time for kid activities—made it difficult for parents like Teresa to participate fully. In fact, another RESULTS volunteer from a decade earlier said that when she announced her decision to adopt a baby, a senior leader immediately told her he was sorry that she would be leaving the group. Back then, it seemed certain that a baby would mean the volunteer would not have time to continue. That decision happened to be right for that particular mom, but Teresa had other ideas. In order to help bend the curve of child deaths toward zero, she was going to have to bend a few rules as well.

Maybe her three Peace Corps years in the Republic of Cameroon had cultivated a resourceful and independent spirit. Maybe she's just a tough mother by nature. Either way, Teresa's persistence kept her in the game.

Instead of hosting regular outreach meetings to invite new members—as RESULTS leadership strongly suggested—Teresa chatted with moms about advocacy as they watched over toddlers at swim lessons or storytime at the library. It was too much to ask those moms to commit to regular meetings, but some of them did show up at meetings occasionally. And that meant Teresa had to create her own instruction manual for handling the toddlers who accompanied them. Her husband stepped up to watch the youngsters and provide them with projects. Every meeting required some activity to keep the kids engaged so parents could think freely for a whole hour. Teresa's group meetings eventually expanded to include feeding everyone potluck-style, giving the meetings a communal family feel.

Teresa simply sidestepped the commitments required to become an "official" group member. RESULTS expected potential members to attend meetings twice a month, take a range of actions, contribute financially, and demonstrate mastery of certain information before they gained official acceptance into the organization. Under her leadership, Teresa's group developed its own expectations: there would be no shaming about levels of commitment; you didn't have to be an all-in member; and any effort to help would be valued by the rest of the group.

Probably influenced by members like Teresa, the RESULTS model evolved to be more welcoming to a variety of lifestyles. Even so, no organization—RESULTS included—will be perfect for every mom's needs. Some advocacy groups hold evening meetings right at peak time for dinner and homework. Others meet on weekends during play rehearsals and soccer games. Some even meet in public places like law firm offices or bars that are not kid-friendly.

I am grateful that I met Teresa early on when I was just beginning to realize that my kid-centered life didn't look like the lives of many of my fellow advocates. I didn't know if a place existed for me in activism anywhere. Teresa told me that mom-advocates have to create a family-friendly schedule even if it isn't business as usual for everyone else. In her coaching, I recognized an experienced advocate who had learned how to juggle life and parenting. She had lived through those moments of speaking with a congressional aide on the phone while a small child kept up a "Mommy Mommy Mommy" chorus in her other ear. Teresa's group spoke to members of Congress and got media published like other groups. They just did it in a way that worked for her family.

Teresa's example proves that mom-advocates can be their own leaders and adapt group models to fit family rhythms. Her work gives moms permission to worry less about doing things the "right" way, according to an organization's guidelines, and focus more on doing things that are right for our kid-filled, paint-splashed lives.

These days we can host online meetings. We can attend web conferences from home or watch recorded webinars when the kids are asleep. Digital freedoms allow participation not only for moms but also for busy college students and people homebound for health reasons. In 2020, everyone came to appreciate the flexibility of doing things in new ways when COVID-19 suddenly required advocacy and most other activities to be carried out digitally and individually.

Teresa eventually became an Advocacy Teams Training Consultant for the Friends Committee on National Legislation. She recruited people to advocate and trained new activists to speak from their heart about peace. Because of her own experiences, she knows it is important to be cognizant of where potential activists are in their own life journeys and what gifts they can share in the moment. "I'm always careful that we celebrate all of the actions that the teammates can bring, whether they brought the salad or took down names at an event. Every single contribution is important to the team. Someone opened up their home. Someone shared a story in a lobby visit that no one else could tell. This attitude is omnipresent when I'm training teams."

Notes

CHAPTER 12

CAN I FIT ADVOCACY INTO MY LIFE?

"How Do You Find the Time?"

That's the question I hear most often when I encourage parents to become advocates. This is a huge concern for parents with children of any age. Whether you are keeping full-time hours at an office, working from home, raising one baby, or wrangling a house full of teenagers, time management is always a challenge. Adding advocacy to the mix, like anything else, is a matter of setting priorities.

We make time for the things that are the most important to us. Education, work, sports, music, religion, and housework all compete for our attention. It's so easy to get caught up in them that we hardly find a moment for ourselves. Take a step back from all your activity calendars and mental to-do lists and to consider these questions:

- ↩ What are you doing for *you*?
- ↩ How are you making the world a better place?
- ↩ What are you doing to help your kids and yourself become more compassionate and caring individuals?

If you think advocacy can help you answer those three questions, then certainly it deserves a place in your family's priorities or at least a slot above "idly surfing the internet." Becoming a world changer isn't going to be so much about *finding* time as it is about *making* time. This is going to be unwelcome news to people who just like to "wing it" each day: you will probably have to become a planner.

Sarah Borgstede, of Belleville, Illinois, is one of the busiest moms I know. She leads an advocacy group, works full-time, and runs all around town supporting her talented kids. She told me, "I realized if I want to have any agency in my life, I'd have to become a planner and expect others around me to plan, too."

Most moms already work all day (whether in an office or at home) and try to create bonding moments with children in the evening. That makes it hard to see how to squeeze in time to become a mom-advocate and save the world. But ask yourself this: "What happens if you *don't* make time to become the best person you want to be?"

Let Your Priorities Set Your Schedule

How do you make time for advocacy? It's all about priorities. I like this anecdote about a teacher giving a time-management lesson. I've seen far too many versions of this to be able to cite an original source, so I'll just include my favorite rendering.

A college professor stood in front of a class with a large, empty beaker and some big rocks. She picked up the rocks and placed as many as she could fit into the beaker and asked the students if the beaker was full. They agreed that it was.

The professor then showed the class a jar of small pebbles and poured them into the beaker, shaking them down to fill in the empty spaces between the rocks. She asked again if the beaker was full. Again, they agreed that it was.

The professor then picked up a box of sand and poured it into the jar. Of course, the sand filled up all remaining spaces between the pebbles. She asked once more if the jar was full. Unanimously, the students told her the beaker was full.

Then, the professor revealed a glass of wine and poured it into the beaker, filling up empty space between the grains of sand. Only then did she let them know the point of the lesson.

She said, "I want you to think of the beaker as representing your life. The big rocks are the important things—family, health, children, friends, and your favorite passions. If you lost everything else, you would think your life was still full as long as you still had them.

"The pebbles are other things that matter—like your job, your house, and your education. The grains of sand are all the tiny other little things that will fill up your life.

"The point is that if you put the sand in first, there will never be room for the pebbles nor the rocks. The same goes for your life. If you spend all your time and energy on the small stuff, you will never have room for the things that are important to you. Pay attention to the things that are critical to your happiness and growth. Play with your kids. Get your medical checkups. Make time for your partner. Learn something new.

"There will always be time to clean the house, throw a party, or play a video game. When you're planning your life, put the big rocks in first—the things that really matter. Set your priorities. The rest is just sand."

One of the students raised a hand and asked about the wine. The professor smiled and said, "I'm glad you asked. It's to show you that no matter how full your life may seem, there's always room for a glass of wine with a friend."

If you think of your life like this, children are definitely some of the "big rocks." Their safety, education, and happiness must be a priority. I view a lot of what I call the "drive-around" activities to be the pebbles. Yes, my kids each have sports or music activities that they love and participate in, and those are important activities to ensure the happiness of my "big rocks." But I cannot fill my beaker only with my children and their activities. When we plan out our family schedule, I place value and importance on my advocacy activities and my personal fitness. It's important for me to figure out how much time I need for them and protect that time.

Advocacy does not have to take over your life or your schedule. Small but important actions can be incorporated into your life with no sacrifice at all. Finding the time to make a two-minute phone call or write a short letter while waiting to pick up your kids from swim practice doesn't require a shifting of priorities but merely the forming of a habit.

You may have to re-examine your priorities again if you decide to increase your advocacy activities or commit to more time-consuming actions. Moving up to the next level will usually come at the cost of more time, but it will often be easier to see the impact of your efforts, which may make you feel more satisfied with how you are spending your time. It can take me an hour to write and submit a few letters to the editor, much longer than it takes to make a few phone calls. But when my letters appear in newspapers and become part of the national discourse, I feel empowered by seeing concrete evidence of my influence. Again, it's all about how you define your priorities.

Whenever a new activity is proposed to the family, my knee-jerk reaction is to say it doesn't fit into the schedule. However, I often have to step back and see how that activity fits into our priorities. My family's schedule gets revisited a few times a year as different sport seasons come and go. Every semester, I get a chance to rearrange the rocks, pebbles, and sand in my beaker, according to our new priorities and needs.

Four Strategies to Make Time for Advocacy

1. Nocturnal Advocacy

This was my first strategy, primarily because my babies would wake me up and I couldn't fall back to sleep. Even when my daughters learned to sleep for longer stretches of time, nighttime was still the right time for advocacy because the fountain of joyful toddler questions made it impossible to sustain any rational train of thought during the day. It's really difficult to be present to a toddler while making thoughtful arguments about government policy at the same time. It's not impossible, but I found it much easier to do quality thinking after their lights were turned off and I'd done the sneaky mommy-check to make sure everyone was quietly breathing in exhausted slumber.

But this strategy can be tricky because you need sleep, too! Sleep is essential for all aspects of your life. If you're going to work late into the night, you need to make time for sleep somewhere else. It's not healthy nor sustainable to work all night long and still be attentive to little ones during the day.

The good news is you don't really need to work the whole night. Fifteen minutes is all it takes to jot down a few handwritten letters to Congress. You might be surprised how fast you can accomplish something when little people aren't asking you questions or demanding more juice.

If you are a stay-at-home mom with napping babies, give yourself permission to take a siesta during the day—especially if you find nighttime advocacy is cutting into your rest. I found that daytime naps often gave me the extra recharge I needed. Plus, I'll never forget the luxurious feeling of snuggling with a sleepy toddler in a sunbeam. It always felt like playing hooky even though it was actually a planned part of my day.

2. Mommy Multitasking

If you have to be at a job early every morning, it would be a horrible idea to burn the candle longer every night. The same is true if you are the kind of person whose brain never functions well past nine p.m. So, let's look at a strategy I call creative "Mommy Multitasking." That's what I call it when I take an activity I was going to do anyway and turn it into an advocacy project.

For instance, perhaps you've made a social commitment to a monthly book club. I used to look forward to those monthly opportunities for grown-up conversation. A few times, I was able to suggest our club read and discuss a book with a global perspective.

Could it enhance your book club to dedicate a month to a book like *Half the Sky* by Nicholas Kristof and Sheryl WuDunn or *I am Malala* by Malala Yousafzai to spur conversations about global girls' education? My church group read *Born a Crime* by comedian Trevor Noah. Not only was it funny, but it also educated us on a perspective of poverty and apartheid from a non-American point of view.

Do your friends sometimes gather for a "Mom's Night Movie?" Whether you're gathering at home or doing an online watch party, you can screen a movie that addresses big issues. It could be a serious documentary-like *13th* about the dangerous loophole in the Thirteenth Amendment that allowed racist policies to persist in the United States. Or it could be a lighter, inspirational film. Disney has a couple of true-life dramas suitable for watching with kids that are great for sparking conversation and action. *Queen of Katwe* is about a Ugandan girl rising out of poverty through education. *McFarland, USA* is a feel-good movie about a high school cross-country team that also engages in topics of racism and community building.

After discussing your book or movie, encourage your group to take a simple action while you are together, such as sending an email or signing up to get more information about a topic. That can allow everyone to leave feeling like they've accomplished something important.

3. In-Between Moments

No matter where we are in life, we always have in-between moments when we can sneak in a little bit of world-saving. And as kids grow older, these moments seem to occur more often and with more predictability for moms.

If you're a brand-new mom with a baby, life often follows an irregular pattern of hours of feeding and diapering and comforting interspersed with pauses that are rarely long enough or predictable enough to plan an outing or get started on a complicated project. Advocacy can fit very logically into them. Nap times are probably the best-known breaks, but they can be a crapshoot for how much time you get. Your cherub could snooze for two hours or pop up after twenty minutes. My kids were entirely unpredictable.

Yet with a little preparation, you can take advantage of even a small amount of alone time. I used to carry around a printed copy of the weekly newsletter for RESULTS in my diaper bag. It included a list of suggested actions for the week, so when the baby was asleep or otherwise occupied, I would pull out my phone and make a call or read up on the global AIDS epidemic. That made me feel more productive and kept me from getting bored if my baby napped unexpectedly or slept for longer than usual.

When you have at least one child in school, the pace of life picks up. But it seems we can never quite shake the "hurry up and wait" holding pattern. Leave work in a whirlwind and then get stuck in traffic. Run, run, run to soccer practice pickup only to find out the coach is keeping them a little longer. Slide into the doctor's office right on time and then wait thirty minutes to be called. Those are great moments to dial up your senators. Leave a short message about an issue you care about, and you will feel far less frustrated about wasted time.

 Tips and Ideas

Tip for calling Congress on the go

Kerry Galson is a high school teacher in the Chicago area. She has her members of Congress on speed dial, so she can call them when she gets delayed on the road. "I don't have time to sit down and write anything anymore. Unfortunately, my challenge is that I have an all-consuming job AND I'm raising three boys. Everything else that isn't my children or my job falls into the margins," she said. "So, I tend to call Congress on my drive after work. I just put whatever office I'm talking to on speaker and explain, 'I'm commuting home!'"

4. Children Included

It seems counterintuitive, but the younger your kids are, the easier it is to work them into certain advocacy steps. I was often able to incorporate a cause into crafts we were doing anyway. That way, the crafts served a purpose and could decorate some other office instead of my way over-decorated kitchen!

While my daughters wrote names with wobbly letters on Valentine cards for classmates, I helped them make a few extra for our members of Congress to remind them to "have a heart" and care about child health. If the kids wanted to do a messy backyard art project, we would put our handprints on a big paper sign about

Girl Scout Daisies in Skokie, IL created a poster for their senator for a "Thinking Day" activity.

early child education and drop it off later for a senator. It doesn't have to be fancy. Big messy posters are very fun to make, and they make an impression! Yes, a kid-crafted advocacy poster given to a congressional office will eventually be tossed, but not before it is noticed by a member of Congress and staff.

As kids grow older, they no longer have much of an appetite for finger painting. However, as they age, it's easier to get them engaged in more advanced actions, such as researching topics, writing letters, or even meeting members of Congress. Kid advocacy can build character and pride in personal success because an advocacy success has real-world results: saving lives, preserving our planet, or easing the suffering of millions. Check out more ideas for advocacy with kids of varying ages in the chapter called "Can Advocacy Make Your Kids' Lives Better?"

Saying No

All this theoretical discussion about priorities is well and good, but in practice, it can be socially difficult to navigate the obligations and opportunities that pop up constantly for a mother, especially once her kids start school. I'm talking about the near-constant requests for moms to run a bake sale, organize a class party, lead a Scouting troop, coach a team, or chair a PTA committee.

Doing a few of these things can be fun. Doing everything that comes your way leads to madness. We have to prioritize what is important to us and learn to gracefully refuse other requests; our time is too precious.

Kids' activities often depend on volunteer involvement, so moms are surrounded by people looking for energy and leadership. If you possess those qualities, you're a hot commodity!

Additionally, if you accept a simple leadership position and perform it well, someone will probably notice and ask for more and more of your time.

To be an effective world changer, you must learn to say "no." Not "I don't think so," or "Well, I'll do it if you can't find someone else," or "Maybe I can squeeze it in." Believe it or not, a good solid "no" can earn you respect and help others value your time.

 ## Tips and Ideas

Tips for saying "no" and accepting "no" from others

"No" doesn't have to mean "not in a million years." Sometimes we treat it that way and that's why we hesitate to say it to friends. We don't want to hurt feelings or shut the door on future opportunities. These three tips help me to be comfortable with the word "no."

- Open your thinking to the idea that "no" could mean "I might be able to do this later when my situation changes." This mindset can be helpful both when you have to decline a request and also when someone refuses your bid for help.
- Offer an alternative. Is there something more in line with your personal goals or less time-consuming you can offer as help?
- Accept that you don't need to give an excuse. "No, but thank you for thinking of me" can be a complete response without embellishment.

I've heard it said of someone in my community, "Boy, she'd be great for that position if you could get on her radar. But she's doing so many things I don't know if she has the time." There was not a hint of bitterness or negativity in the comment. No one was going to be personally insulted if that mom didn't join in because they knew that if she actually said "yes," she'd be committed and turn down other opportunities that would distract her.

On the other hand, I've known plenty of women who say "yes" to so many things that they miss meetings, forget deadlines, and drop important tasks. They're well-meaning, but not reliable. I know this type of woman well because I have been one. We all want to be dependable, but we can become untrustworthy if we're not vigilant about our priorities and what opportunities we accept.

🕐 Story 📖 time!

Jennifer DeFranco of Palatine, Illinois, has often wrestled with the dilemma of overcommitting to her volunteer opportunities. She's been a valuable volunteer with Shot@Life, PTA, Girl Scouts, youth soccer, church activities, a local homeless shelter, and her own family's foundation. "When you have spent years saying yes to volunteer roles because you felt guilty or because you were afraid you might let someone down, the word 'no' becomes a word you don't say very often."

When Jennifer did finally turn down a big request for her help, she struggled with the decision. "I nearly retracted my answer and told them 'yes' before it was all said and done, but I didn't. I will admit it felt pretty good—even liberating! Taking control and evaluating my own time and reasons was exactly what I needed to do."

She now determines where her time will have the most impact and has chosen to let some things go because she believes they weren't accomplishing much for the missions she believes in. "I've spent far too many hours knee-deep in drama when those hours could have been spent doing something that really mattered, something that could actually change a life.

"In the end," said Jennifer, "there is only so much time each of us has and we have to choose to use it for what we feel is best for us, not them."

Advocacy Can Equal Self-Care

I believe many things—including motherhood—are best in moderation. Mothering involves taking care of the most important people in our lives. Yet we still have to ensure we make room in our lives for self-care even if it takes a little extra time. Any flight attendant will tell you to put on your oxygen mask first to make sure your body functions well enough to secure masks on your children. Making sure we have what we need first actually makes us better mothers.

When we talk about self-care, we are usually referring to getting plenty of rest, eating healthy foods, and getting exercise. I don't want any mother to neglect those necessities. But I also want you to consider activities that lead to personal growth and increased self-esteem as self-care. Advocating for changes you believe in can provide precious fuel for your mind and soul which you need in order to nurture the minds and souls of your children.

Maxine Thomas is a mom of five in Indianapolis who knows a thing or two about getting run down and tired. She said, "Believe it or not, advocacy gives me a sense of therapy when I feel bad about what's happening around me. So, taking action is really uplifting!"

It's Your Turn!

1. With which friends would you feel most comfortable discussing social issues? In what setting would you feel most comfortable talking about such topics?

2. Are there any issue-related books you've read or been meaning to read that might be better if digested with a group of friends? What about movies?

3. What are the big rocks in your life? What parts of your life can be thought of as filler sand, taking away from what you want to do?

4. Do you have small pockets of time in your life where you could fit in a phone call to Congress or a quick letter? When do you have bigger blocks of time?

5. Do you have trouble saying "no" to requests for your time and energy? Why or why not?

Notes

Yolanda Gordon

Photo credit: RESULTS Educational Fund.

CHAPTER 13

PROFILE: YOLANDA GORDON MANAGING TIME AND ENERGY

WHEN I TALK ABOUT my advocacy work with other moms, conversations usually begin this way:

"It's great you have so much free time to work on something like this."

"I could never do what you do because I work a full-time job."

"My kids take up all of my energy, so I don't see how I could do that."

There's no doubt that elements of my life make it easier for me to do my advocacy work. But stay-at-home suburban moms with kids in school are not the only mothers who find time and resources to advocate. Indeed, some of the most powerful mom-advocates I know are in the thick of raising their children and struggling with systems stacked against them. They have little spare time and less spare energy. Yet they speak out because they understand nothing will ever change on its own. Yolanda Gordon is one of those powerful world changers.

Yolanda is one of the most confident and determined women I have ever met. She has a quick sense of humor yet is not swift to laugh; she has little energy to waste for trivialities. If Yolanda ever tells you that she has no time for you, take it as a brutally honest assessment of her own scheduling capacity. She joined the military at age seventeen, so she learned early on that directness is a necessary tool for getting through demanding days.

When Yolanda and I attended advocacy conferences together in 2015, she was a thirty-five-year-old single mom of three kids with developmental challenges. Her fifteen-year-old daughter had been diagnosed as bipolar, her eleven-year-old son as autistic, and her nine-year-old daughter with Asperger's syndrome. Yet Yolanda was finishing up a degree in occupational therapy with a 3.92 GPA from Central Piedmont Community College in South Carolina and advocating for more causes than you can shake a stick at. On the side, she was also starting a community garden to feed hungry people in her neighborhood.

Yolanda doesn't believe advocates need to focus on just one cause. She has no problem advocating fiercely for several issues, whenever and wherever things need doing. She began her advocacy journey while raising three neurodiverse children by speaking out for their educational rights. She also takes on people who blame autism on vaccines without real medical proof, stating boldly, "Yes, my son has autism and he did *not* get it from a vaccine, thank you very much." Because she has lived in poverty while serving as the sole breadwinner for her family, she shares firsthand experiences when she stands up for tax credits for low-income workers and for programs that help feed hungry folks in our nation.

How does such a colossally busy mother have time for activism? She does much of it during the "in-between" moments. "I could be sitting and having a cup of coffee and I can just quickly shoot an email to my Congressman's office that says, 'Hey, thanks for supporting the UN Foundation's Shot@Life. Let's keep supporting global vaccines. And while you're looking at this, let's look at X, Y, and Z as well.'"

Yolanda also prefers to compartmentalize her activism activities by action type. "I have a day during the month when I write my emails. I have a day during the month that I make my phone calls. It's my focus that day. I don't care if I don't get the staffer that I want to talk to, I'll just leave my message. I've been in touch so much that they already have my contact info. So when I call, they'll email back just to tell me, 'I got your message.'"

She wants other moms to recognize that they really do have time for advocacy if they recognize how important it is. "I express, especially to moms with special needs kids who tell me they don't have time, that it is really a matter of life or death for your child. Think about all the things that your child needs that the government is cutting right now that may not be fixed later. You have to make time."

Advocacy is very personal for Yolanda because she feels like people on Capitol Hill typically see only one side of many issues. She wants to bring the other side to them. Hers is a much-needed voice on Capitol Hill, describing what it was like for her family to depend on government programs while she worked toward better opportunities. It's impossible for anyone to argue that she is not a hard worker, and her military experience underscores her dedication to making the U.S. a better place for all Americans.

One staffer told Yolanda that the nutrition program they were discussing should be more like the Women, Infant, and Children (WIC) program. "Have you ever personally known someone to get WIC?" she challenged. The staffer admitted he did not. Yolanda promised, "I'm going to send you an email with a list of everything you can get with WIC and you tell me if what people need through food stamps would be covered in that. It's cheese. It's juice. It's just a supplement. It's not enough for complete nutrition."

Yolanda followed up and sent the list as promised. In response, the aide sent her a handwritten letter thanking her for clarifying the program and shining a light on how real people use assistance programs. Yolanda had provided an important perspective the office did not have to advise the member in making decisions.

I won't say that Yolanda is a boundless fountain of energy. She gets tired. Bone tired. "Mom is tired seventy-five percent of the time," she admitted about herself. It's emotionally draining for her to advocate with congressional offices knowing she's working against a mental image they have about single Black mothers. She said, "It's like there's this granite wall, and you're standing on the other side of it. You have to chip away at it to get the person on the other side to see you as a human, as a person, as someone who is just doing the best that they can to survive."

But she continually stretches the limits of her endurance in advocacy because she believes it's the morally right thing to do and the best thing for her children. The way she sees it, every time she stands up for her values, she is helping her children. She is working to create a system where it will be possible for her kids and kids like them to get what they need and deserve. She is also helping them by setting an example of grit and good character.

"My son was a beautiful little boy," Yolanda said. "His principal pulled him aside and she said to him, 'Your mom's a Gordon.

You're a Gordon. You don't give up. She doesn't give up.'" She was satisfied to watch her son shift from "I can't do this" to "I'm going to try" just because someone had told him, "Your mom doesn't give up." Her model of perseverance shaped the young man he is today.

Her son isn't the only one to benefit from her example these days. Yolanda eventually changed her career to work full-time on advocacy. Now, as Manager of Expansion and Advocacy with RESULTS, she coaches hundreds of college students on an advocacy fellowship.

Ultimately, Yolanda finds overcoming all the emotional challenges and scheduling hurdles in her activism worth the effort. "It is exhausting, but it's gratifying when you get that random email or call saying, 'Hey, we discussed this last year. I wanted to circle back and talk to you about it.' When you hear that it's like, 'Yessss!' Don't think that that will not happen. That's the gratification."

Notes

CHAPTER 14

STEP OUT OF YOUR COMFORT ZONE

ARE YOU UNCOMFORTABLE WITH the idea of becoming an activist? That's a natural reaction when you're challenged with something new. There is nothing wrong and everything right about starting your activism with the action that feels most comfortable to you.

Yet a funny thing happens when you step out of your comfort zone. Most of the time, you end up realizing that it wasn't as bad as you expected it would be. And even if it is that bad, you start feeling stronger when you realize you can do it anyway!

Bit by bit, I was encouraged to become a more powerful advocate by taking actions that challenged me. I continue to feel nervous—and maybe even a little nauseated—whenever I make a bold new move. Yet I now have the experience of knowing that the cold feeling in my stomach doesn't last, and I become more powerful with every new experience.

⏱ Story 📖 time!

Making phone calls to elected officials makes Jennifer Burden, founder of World Moms Network, uncomfortable. Jennifer advocates for global access to immunizations and also for U.S. vaccine policy. She enjoys sharing her views in face-to-face meetings and wouldn't hesitate to sit down with a senator. However, a day came when a phone call was the fastest, most effective way to advocate, and she found that task much harder for her than any office visit.

In the midst of U.S. measles outbreaks in 2015, New Jersey governor Chris Christie declared that vaccine decisions should be left up to the judgment of parents instead of the government. Jennifer lives in New Jersey and believes that vaccines should not be optional for measles. Because of her work with Every Child By Two—an organization advocating for vaccines for American children (now known as Vaccinate Your Family)—she felt well-informed and outraged at his remarks.

As Christie's constituent, she was one of the few people in the country who could even leave a message that his office would accept. Yet the phone call intimidated her, despite all of her in-person advocacy experiences. "I am very comfortable reading and responding to body language during an in-person discussion. It is like a super-power that I can't use in a phone conversation!"

Nevertheless, she knew the phone was the best way to get her message across in that moment, so she made the call to her governor's office. Her heart was racing as an aide noted her comment. "I felt so empowered afterward. During the call, I was so nervous. I kept thinking, 'What if I get Chris Christie himself on the phone?'"

Jennifer knew in her head that the governor wouldn't personally answer his main office line, but her irrational fear still felt very real as she dialed the numbers.

Ultimately, she decided the uneasiness she would feel on the line with an office assistant would be far easier than the suffering of a child who needlessly contracted measles. She drew courage from thinking of children in our country who could not have vaccines for various medical reasons—newborns and kids with immunity issues—and who needed the protection of herd immunity. Because she empathizes strongly with mothers of those children at risk, she accepted her own discomfort for their sake.

Jennifer Burden changed her Facebook profile picture to this confident image after making her first advocacy phone call.
Photo credit: Jennifer Burden.

Shortly after she made the call, she changed her Facebook profile image to a photo of herself standing at a podium. She wanted the whole world to see her as she saw herself: a strong woman not afraid to speak her mind. "I want to be that girl in the picture, so confident and secure!"

What kinds of uncomfortable things have you done for your own child that you wouldn't have previously dreamed of doing for anyone else? Dressed up in a silly costume? Used a rectal thermometer? Maybe it's a personal act of bravery, like the time I kept smiling at my baby so she wouldn't freak out while I removed a spider from the side of her face with my bare hand.

Every day, moms engage in uncomfortable acts to help our children. We stand up to teachers and coaches if they don't have our kids' best interests in mind. We confront parents of other children who bully our own. For your child, you can find within yourself the strength to move mountains. Could you tap into this same source of strength just to make a phone call or sit down at a meeting, if you knew it could benefit millions of children? For the sake of suffering children and mothers, I conquered my fear of meeting a member of Congress. For them, I found the courage to ask my friends to give at fundraisers. For them, I'm battling my own insecurities about my ability to write a book because I hope I can convince you to use your energies and talents to make our world better and safer for all of us.

Put Yourself Out There

I have found that many mothers hesitate to reach out and engage others on matters that might seem political in any way. We tend to think that others won't find these issues as interesting or important as we do. We are afraid that friends might be offended by our position or feel we are judging them. Or we worry that people will think an "advocacy meeting" will be like one of those TV news shows where people yell about politics and call each other names.

Let's face it. Most of the things we're talking about—poverty, climate change, violence—are uncomfortable to confront and think about. But we need to talk to others to create momentum and reinspire ourselves.

Advocacy coach Ken Patterson of RESULTS once told me, "If you feel a queasy, cold feeling in your stomach, it probably means you're doing the right thing." Of course, there are exceptions to this characterization: this advice does *not* apply to walking alone through a dark parking garage. Still, I think the most valuable kinds of growth are inherently going to be a bit uncomfortable. Advocacy is no exception.

 Tips and Ideas

Tips to help overcome nervousness

- If you experience a racing pulse and heavy breathing when you take an advocacy action, you totally get to consider that as a cardio workout for the day!

- Remind yourself that actions get easier and less stressful every time you do them. Like riding a bike or driving a car, things that make us nervous can become routine skills we use to move forward in life.

Facing Uncomfortable Realities

Most readers of a book addressed to mothers have likely encountered some incidents of sexism. Perhaps men have talked over you in meetings or "mansplained" concepts to you. It's an awful feeling to have your ideas discounted or ignored, especially when you're going out on a limb to exercise your personal power.

People of many historically oppressed groups frequently encounter such condescension, but perhaps none deal with it more keenly or more regularly than women of color. Activists who are Black, Indigenous, and People of Color (BIPOC) face added hurdles of negative stereotypes and microaggressions, and they regularly encounter discouraging, preconceived ideas from members of Congress or staff during in-person meetings. We can all learn about dealing with such frustrations from the wisdom of some BIPOC mom-advocates.

Although the incoming 117th Congress of 2021 included more women and people of color than any previous Congress, about seventy-five percent of those members were white. Having visited Capitol Hill for more than fifteen years, I've seen that most congressional staffers are also white. In 2020, only about eleven percent of top Senate staff members—including chiefs of staff, legislative directors, and communications directors—were people of color.[15] People in these positions regularly influence decisions, shape policy, and in some cases speak or write as surrogate senators. Such imbalance means mom-advocates who are not white are likely to encounter racial bias at some point.

I don't call out these statistics to dishearten you or scare you away from advocacy. Instead, I want to highlight the urgent need for real constituents to fill important conversations with underrepresented voices. Our leaders need to hear truth delivered by women with lived experience, especially when they are considering issues that arise from inequalities and systemic racism in our country.

Having their stories dismissed outright or hearing backhanded compliments such as, "You're so articulate!" can be exhausting. So, what compels BIPOC mom-advocates to keep going? Let's read some of their own words.

> I'm a Black, single mother going to offices to talk about my experience living in poverty. It's draining to have to break that ice and have that conversation, knowing they are still going to look at you and shake their head. But I'm much bolder going in there because of the relationships I've built over time. I've been to my senator's office and met his staff so many times that I feel like they know me now. Like, really know me.
>
> —Maxine Thomas, Indianapolis, Indiana

> It took me a while to feel the power of a mom speaking in the office, but now it feels like the greatest thing. It's not the easiest thing. I feel really proud. We've done meetings completely in

---

[15] L. Brenson, "Racial Diversity Among Top Staff in Senate Personal Offices," Joint Center for Political and Economic Studies, August 2020.

Spanish. It's indescribable. It keeps me motivated for the next time.

—Columba Sainz, Phoenix, Arizona

I probably shouldn't think like this, but it's like, "I'm gonna prove you wrong. I am someone. I'm not just a stereotype of what you see or hear as an African American woman." When I tell my story over and over again, it's very emotional. It's exhausting because I'm not too keen on being vulnerable. But just the fact that my story will help someone, or that my story will be an inspiration or enlighten whoever I'm talking to makes me feel like, "If you're willing to listen and make this count, then I'm willing to tell you." If my story can inspire someone else, I'll tell it 1000 times.

—Candace Ellis, Belleville, Illinois

 Tips and Ideas

Tips to help white moms support BIPOC mom-advocates

It's bad enough when BIPOC activists face racism or condescension from members of Congress or their staff, but it's even worse if they confront the same issues with their own advocacy partners. Even though it feels uncomfortable at first, it's important for white mom-advocates to confront their own biases and attitudes when partnering with advocates from other races or ethnic groups. Good allies will not perpetuate racist attitudes or policies.

This issue is complex, but here are a few suggestions to start white readers in the right direction.

- Read to educate yourself on privilege, racism, and microaggressions so you recognize when your partners confront those problems. You can't support them very well if you don't understand how they have been oppressed.
- Apologize immediately, without making any excuses, if you discover you have hurt someone with your words or actions. Ask politely for a time to listen to the person so you can understand and not repeat the mistake, but don't be resentful if they don't want to discuss it with you. It's not their job to educate you.
- Consider "passing the microphone" to a BIPOC mom-advocate if you are offered a chance to speak in public or write for a publication. It will help make those opportunities more available to others and let audiences hear more diverse perspectives.

Choose How You Want to Advocate

As you consider all the advice you encounter in this book, think of the suggested actions as potential ingredients in a recipe for your advocacy. You're going to come up with your own individual blend of ingredients that is right for you. If you are a people person, you might prefer actions that involve a more personal touch, including face-to-face meetings and actions. If your only available time comes at night when your family is asleep, start with actions you can take when congressional offices are closed.

My own advocacy mix has drawn from all of these suggestions at one time or another. What I did with middle-schoolers would not have worked when I was a toddler-wrangler. We moms have to be improvisational chefs who work with the resources we have on hand at the moment.

Most advocacy organizations have a particular formula that grows out of their history and culture. An organization that started as an online community may insist their members promote and participate in online campaigns. Another organization may consider face-to-face lobbying the only worthwhile action. Whether you flex the norms of those communities or find an organization specifically suited to your style, find a recipe that amplifies your strengths. My favorite mom-advocates never seem to play strictly by other people's rules or schedules. They just find what works in advocacy, much like they do in parenting.

Rest easy in the knowledge that I'm offering general guidelines, not hard and fast rules to make your life more difficult. Just as you discovered that no parenting book could anticipate all your individual circumstances, you'll see that you can find your own path after following this guide in the right general direction. Bring your own creativity and unique flavor to your actions; that's what makes it both fun and possible.

It's Your Turn!

1. What kinds of uncomfortable things have you done for your own child that you wouldn't have previously dreamed of doing for anyone else? What kinds of things have you done for friends' children? What would you do for children you will never meet?

2. Are there activities that used to make you uncomfortable but are easy now because you have done them frequently? Can

those experiences give you confidence that advocacy actions will grow easier over time?

3. If you knew you could change things for the better, what discomfort would you be willing to face?

4. Do you avoid situations of racial tension? What resources (books, friends, mentors, podcasts, etc.) can you find to help you confront your discomfort?

5. How does racial inequality affect your advocacy issue? Could you prepare to discuss this with other advocates or congressional offices?

Laura Frisch

Photo credit: Laura Frisch.

CHAPTER 15

PROFILE: LAURA FRISCH
BUILDING COMMUNITY

ALTHOUGH I HAVE KNOWN Laura Frisch for more than fifteen years, I remain amazed at how she uses every opportunity to exponentially grow efforts for good and to build up the community around her in positive ways. Frankly, I both admire and fear her abilities because she pushes the boundaries of my own comfort zone. Knowing Laura has made me a bolder organizer.

As a mom of young children, Laura skillfully created a fun and welcoming community for her friends and neighbors; she carried those skills into her local schools and later into troubled Chicago neighborhoods. Now she works to foster a nationwide community that can create a safer place for all.

When we were both raising little ones in Morton Grove, Illinois, Laura's house was a swirling epicenter of neighborhood activity. Two kids and four dogs made for a bustling home on the quietest of days, and her door was always open to welcome friends and their kids for anything from an impromptu backyard picnic to a messy tie-dye T-shirt session.

To Laura, anything worth doing with two friends was worth doing with ten friends! She was so comfortable in the chaos that her first instinct was always to ask, "How can we include more people? How do we make this open and accessible for everyone?" This tendency was both a challenge and an inspiration to an introvert like me, who generally wanted to keep things comfortable and cozy for myself. Yet I knew that whenever I wanted to rally the Morton Grove community, Laura was the secret ingredient for cooking up any of my schemes.

For example, I once thought it would be good to replace the school's annual wrapping paper fundraiser with a walkathon so our kids could do something healthy instead of generating more disposable waste. I laid my idea at Laura's feet. Before I knew it, we had a school day set aside for a walkathon and a volunteer committee of parents scurrying to find sponsors, collect donations, and judge a T-shirt design contest.

Laura didn't stop there. She arranged for a school for students with emotional or physical challenges to participate in our walkathon and to share in the proceeds, too. That school had significant financial needs but no parent organization to raise money. Laura took my idea and made it bigger. More inclusive. More accessible.

I moved away from Illinois in 2013, but I kept in touch with Laura, and I wasn't surprised when she became involved with a nationwide advocacy group in the aftermath of the 2012 Sandy Hook Elementary School shooting. Laura, who had been teaching a park district preschool class on the day of the shooting, said, "It was like Pearl Harbor Day. I distinctly remember I was working in one of those little one-room schoolhouses. No protection there. I thought about how I've had incidents where divorced parents tried to pick up kids without authority and I had to call the police." In those times of conflict, it had only been Laura and two helpers caring for fifteen preschoolers. No security backup.

The thought of what could happen if an armed person came with the intent to harm her or her class prompted her to join the Facebook group of Shannon Watts, an Indiana stay-at-home mom who felt compelled to take action after the Sandy Hook massacre. Shannon started a nationwide discussion among mothers about how Americans could and should do more to reduce gun violence.

This impromptu group went viral and eventually became Moms Demand Action for Gun Sense in America. It's now a widespread grassroots movement of Americans who are fighting for public safety measures to reduce gun violence. Members advocate for stronger gun laws and work to close loopholes that jeopardize public safety. They also work in their own communities and with business leaders to encourage a culture of responsible gun ownership.

Nowadays, Moms Demand Action is an advocacy juggernaut that inspires seas of supporters in red T-shirts to descend upon state legislatures to promote "gun-sense" legislation. The organization has at least one chapter in every state and nearly six million supporters. But Laura was there in the early days when Moms Demand Action consisted of small pockets of moms around the country who were simply trying to start conversations about gun safety.

"We were a total ragtag little team of people who started out saying, 'Let's talk about it at our PTO meetings' and turned it into 'Let's find out how to lobby,'" she recalled. At the time, she had no idea how big the movement would become or that she would bring the Moms Demand organization to the whole North Shore area of Chicago.

In addition to Laura, several Moms Demand members lived in Chicago or its suburbs, and one of them learned a mother had been killed while protecting her child from a drive-by shooting. So, a couple of nearby members went to sit in solidarity with neighbors on the Englewood corner where that mother had been shot.

Laura believes it's important to know that Moms Demand volunteers went with a spirit of partnership to places where allies were already working against gun violence, rather than simply showing up after a shooting for a photo op. "It's more like, when there was a group there already, they'd say, 'Come and help,' and we'd show up to support each other."

In Englewood, what began as a small vigil on a corner started by Tamar Manasseh of MASK, Mothers and Men Against Senseless Killings, soon blossomed into a regular event the community could count on for safety. The gatherings went like this: Take charcoal and food for seventy-five people to a local park. Bring along a local Lutheran pastor, Islamic leaders, and Jewish congregants. Get together and talk to people in a block-party setting. Feed everyone.

The atmosphere was energizing and loving. On these block party nights, kids in the neighborhood knew this would be a safe spot where they could get something to eat, which was important because many of the kids were food insecure. Laura would set up a face-painting table, something she often did for events at her synagogue and the Morton Grove Farmers' Market. Her face painting gave kids a chance to sit down with a safe adult for one-on-one time, helping them build positive memories of being a kid.

Moms Demand volunteers in Chicago continue to work with local groups organizing these kinds of gatherings to provide whatever is needed. They strive to make these areas feel safer and to help children escape the fear they carry with them. Members also listen to kids tell stories of the people they have lost.

Laura's role with Moms Demand Action grew as the organization addressed more state and national initiatives, including speaking to legislators and supporting a campaign to spread safety awareness among gun owners. But she still makes time to go back to that same Englewood gathering, which never stopped trying to make that corner a safe place to be. Even though MASK runs the event on its own, Laura still goes twice a year, bringing more people with her each time.

"It's hot and there's very little shade," Laura admitted. "It's a schlep down there, but we go back every year. Every single time I'm thinking, 'This is affecting people in a positive way,' so I keep going."

When she reflected upon how the organization has expanded from the eclectic group of volunteers who gathered in the early days, Laura said, "Moms Demand was the sorority everyone could join. Of course, it's serious business. Many people joined because they lost a child or loved one to gun violence, so it wasn't all fun with sisters. But everyone was welcome."

Baking this kind of inclusiveness into the organization's culture has helped it grow and gain power. With a problem as widespread as gun violence, it's important to get all kinds of allies on board to create and run safety campaigns and encourage the election of gun-sense candidates. They may have started as a bunch of moms, but those moms knew they needed to enlist the help of dads, kids, hunters, gun-toting grandmas, members of Congress, and even conservative news pundits.

Not long after my 2019 conversation with Laura, conservative CNN host S. E. Cupp—nationally known as an outspoken supporter of the National Rifle Association (NRA)—announced on air that she had dropped her NRA membership in the wake of mass shootings in El Paso, Texas, and Dayton, Ohio. In an impassioned speech, she spoke in favor of legislative measures that Moms Demand advocates had promoted for years: universal background checks, bans on the sale of large drums of ammunition, and measures to prevent domestic abusers from having access to guns. Just four years earlier, Cupp had appeared in an advertisement as a self-proclaimed "NRA mom" who urged others to join the NRA. I don't know whether Cupp will join Moms Demand, but I think she would find that sorority accepting of her.

Building movements and organizing volunteers is hard. It can be messy when a lot of different personalities and viewpoints clash. But changing the world takes a wide diversity of voices and personalities, and we don't always get to pick and choose who shows up to help. Laura understands that if we work only with people who look like us, shop like us, worship like us, and play like us, then we are not going to change much of anything at all. Her solution is to welcome everybody.

When I asked what drives her sense of inclusivity, Laura denied suggestions that it came from her religion or early role models. Instead, she said, "I was lonely as a kid. I'm never going to make someone not be included. I've stood in those shoes and I'm not going to make anyone else stand in them."

Most of us have felt lonely and left out at times in our lives. Let's channel those feelings as Laura does to make others feel more comfortable as we work together. Building inclusive movements is the greatest gift we can share to take powerful actions and help more people.

CHAPTER 16

WHAT'S STOPPING YOU FROM BECOMING AN ADVOCATE?

MOST OF OUR HESITATION to begin comes from a fear of the unknown. If you simply don't know what to do, read the step-by-step instructions and stories waiting for you in "Part III: Advocacy Made Easy." You will feel more empowered and less worried by the time you reach the end of that section.

But maybe your hesitation is rooted in something deeper. If so, I invite you to step back and ask yourself:

- ◄) What is preventing me from taking action right now?
- ◄) How much am I risking if I make a phone call to Congress or schedule a meeting with an aide in a congressional office?
- ◄) What am I afraid of?

Now, weigh your fears about potential consequences of you taking action against what might happen if you do nothing. What is at risk for the world if people like us don't speak out? Girls in poverty will continue to grow up oppressed and uneducated. Infants will continue to die of *almost*-eradicated diseases like polio and illnesses that are easily prevented in wealthy nations. Parents in poverty will struggle to feed their families. American children will continue to lose their lives to gun violence. Families will suffer from asthma caused by poor air quality.

Our fears tend to shrink when we compare our temporary emotional discomforts against what happens when we don't step out to defend and protect the most vulnerable among us.

If you're scared to advocate, take comfort in the knowledge that pretty much everyone feels the same way at first! When you are feeling weak and insecure, imagine one person who can be helped by your actions and find your strength there. Concentrating on one specific mother or child who needs you can feel more energizing than thinking of nameless, faceless millions.

A lot of people find themselves paralyzed by a few common fears, so let's look at some of those.

I'm Afraid I'll Make a Mistake

Are you afraid of getting your facts wrong on a phone call? Making typos in an email? Accidentally thanking your member of Congress for something they didn't actually do? Well, I've done all those things, and I'm here to say I survived! Not only that, I'm a better advocate and leader because of my mistakes.

Overcoming the fear of making mistakes requires some inner strength and sometimes support from trusted mentors. But here are two pieces of good news about mistakes.

1. **Every mistake you make is a learning opportunity.** We learn from our mistakes. Isn't that what we tell our children? I reminded my kids of that often when they learned to ice skate. If you never fall down, that's a sign you're not trying hard and learning as much as you can.

2. **A mistake can be a blessing in disguise.** Sometimes our mistakes remind staffers in a good way that we are ordinary volunteer citizens and not paid lobbyists. Most of them are aware that it's a courageous act for us to contact them and are very forgiving of miscues or fumbled explanations. After all, you must really care a lot about an issue if you make a mistake and then call back to correct it. If you're polite about causing an inconvenience, it could lead to an even better personal relationship with the aide!

You definitely won't be alone in making a typo or slip of the tongue. I've seen so many intelligent global activists make the silly, honest mistake of mixing up the words "millions" and "billions." As you can imagine, it makes a big difference whether one million people are at risk for a disease or one billion! If you went to a global advocacy conference and asked a couple hundred volunteer activists if any of them had ever made that error, I bet about half of them would raise their hands. Probably another quarter either wouldn't admit it or just never noticed when they made the mistake.

When my CARE group was on a phone conference call with a Senate aide asking for $12 billion dollars in international funding to fight the COVID-19 pandemic, I made that classic goof of asking for only $12 million. That might sound like a lot of money to the average citizen, but to the Senate, that's a tiny drop in the bucket!

Fortunately, I had already emailed the aide a document with the correct amount and the group discussed the specifics during a thirty-minute conversation. She could readily see that $900 million for vaccines and $250 million for nutrition wasn't going to fit into my measly $12 million request. There are very few mistakes that can't be corrected, especially when you're doing the deep sort of advocacy that involves back-and-forth conversations, teamwork, and building personal relationships with members of Congress and their staff. Six months later, $11.55 billion in global assistance was included in the next COVID-19 relief bill, so I know for a fact that the fate of the world did not hang on my mistake!

What should you do if you make a mistake that doesn't get corrected in a meeting? Exactly the same thing we tell our children to do if they mess up:

- Admit you made a mistake
- Apologize
- Correct it as best you can
- Do your very best to avoid similar mistakes in the future

At any given moment, there will be news reports of members of Congress apologizing for something they did, said, or tweeted. Sometimes the apology is for something illegal. Sometimes for something immoral. Sometimes it's just for clumsily saying the wrong thing at the wrong time. Whatever it is, it more than proves that our elected officials are human, too.

Story time!

Sarah Borgstede, RESULTS volunteer and busy mom in Illinois, made what turned out to be a very fortunate error while advocating for global education. She was trying to ask her representative to sign onto House Resolution 466 to support the Global Partnership for Education. That resolution, an official statement reflecting a position held by members of Congress, was abbreviated as "H. Res. 466," but Sarah accidentally wrote "H.R. 466" in her request. "H.R." stands for "House of Representatives" and indicates a bill that could become an actual binding law.

Sarah was very surprised to receive a form letter from Congressman Mike Bost saying that he would indeed vote for H.R. 466 if it came to a vote because he opposed human trafficking. She thought, "Great! But . . . what?" Turns out that H.R. 466 was a bill called the "Sex Trafficking Demand Reduction Act." While happy that her congressman opposed sex trafficking, Sarah was embarrassed that she had accidentally asked him to support the wrong piece of legislation!

Swallowing her pride, she called up the aide in the office to admit the error and asked if she could come into the office to explain what H. Res. 466 was about. Not only did the aide grant her request, but he scheduled her to meet with Congressman Bost himself. Sarah got a face-to-face meeting on the calendar mainly because she made a mistake and had the grace to quickly follow up on it.

I'm Afraid I Can't Answer Questions

I was extremely worried about this when I first started. Now, it's the last thing that I worry about. Why? Certainly not because I know all the answers!

First of all, when you are leaving a phone message, chances are slim that anyone will contact you with a follow-up question about your position. Congressional offices get far too many letters, emails, and phone messages to answer each one. Generally, the staffer receiving your message will simply log the contact and note whether you are for or against an issue. You don't have to compose elaborate responses to a counterargument.

When you are in a real-time exchange, a question you can't answer is a real gift! All you need to do is to reply, "That's a great question! I don't know, but I can find out and get back to you." The question you can't answer on the spot is like an invitation to communicate with the office again. Afterward, when the pressure is off, you can find out what you didn't know.

In a meeting, your primary mission as a volunteer is to make a personal connection and tell your congressional office why you care. You're not expected to give a legal briefing. I often adjust expectations right up front by letting my contact know that I am a volunteer. It sets a good tone immediately and buys some goodwill.

 ## Tips and Ideas

Tips for responding when you don't have answers

I keep these responses in my back pocket in case a member of Congress or an aide stumps me in a meeting, which happens more than you might think.

- "I don't know offhand, but I'm happy to find out for you."
- "That's a great question. Can I do a little research and get back to you?"
- "No one has ever asked me that before. I'd love to check on that and let you know next week."

I'm Afraid I Will Fail

We are each responsible for setting our own expectations for what success and failure look like. I have decided that if I speak up for my issue honestly and sincerely, then I have advocated successfully.

Do I always get instant agreement or action from the people I talk to? No. Not always. Not even usually. But failure to get a "yes" from your member of Congress on a particular day is not necessarily a failure. Most advocacy is like running a marathon, not a sprint. Some bills do move quickly and are passed in a year. Others, like the "READ Act," the first bill I worked on promoting global education, take a decade or more to pass.

Your actions might fail to have the immediate effect you want yet turn out to make a difference down the road. This can happen when your representative seems unmoved by your request, but the story you tell greatly touches the heart of a staffer in the meeting who will eventually support your cause when she goes to work for your senator in the future (that exact staffing scenario happened to me). So, don't be too hard when judging your performance.

Yolanda Gordon often meets in offices that don't agree with her requests about nutrition and housing assistance for low-income Americans. She said, "You have to go through that journey to get to that moment to say, 'You know what? There's no way for me to fail.' All I can do is go and tell my truth, tell them what we need, walk out, and just be confident in what I did in that moment. Then, just let that sit." I agree. Speak truth to power and you will be able to claim success.

Story time!

Andrea Riley, a mom and former volunteer leader for the Shot@Life campaign from Lincoln, Nebraska, learned a helpful lesson about measuring success when she was a middle-school runner.

> Close the gap. On my first long-distance race in seventh-grade track, my coach told me 'Don't worry about beating all the other girls, just focus on closing the gap between you and the girl in front of you.' It took the pressure off, gave me a realistic goal to work for, and made running much more fun. Instead of being about winning and losing, it's about the importance of making incremental gains and holding onto them—that's the only way progress is made. I find this is especially important with the broader and stickier problems in life, where change can be frustratingly slow.
>
> In advocacy, focus on creative ways to close the gap between where you are and where you want to be. If one of those ways isn't working, don't sweat it, just try a different approach. Be constantly building and strengthening relationships; this will get you far. Also have patience, because lasting change takes time, so celebrate every small victory you get along the way.

I'm Afraid It's All Too Much

It's okay if the more advanced advocacy actions seem very far away from your current abilities and available time. Do what you can do at the moment of doing. Advocacy is available to you even if you have just a tiny bit of time, and it does not have to be an all-consuming, daily pursuit.

If the not-so-simple act of bundling your munchkins up to go to the grocery store led to tears today, it's probably not a good day to try a new advocacy skill. Wait for a moment when you feel like you need to protect your children's future. When you're in that mindset, go for it!

Your mommy work is important. Don't let anyone tell you anything different. It needs to come first. I'm the first person to urge moms to take a plunge and try something new, but you must pick a time that is right and an action that is inspiring to you. Becoming an advocate is a series of small steps and big leaps. Saying yes to do one easy thing does not oblige you to do harder things right away, or ever. Just because you "sign on" to do one thing, like writing a short letter, you're in no way required to do everything listed in Part III of this book.

Just pick one action and give yourself permission to only stick to the thing you've agreed to try. Say "no" to yourself and others when you must. Make boundaries and keep your commitments manageable in order to be the kind of mother—the kind of person—you want to be. Don't allow the fact that you can't do everything to keep you from doing something. Something is better than nothing!

I'm Not Afraid of Anything . . . I Just Don't Have a Babysitter

I hear you. I've been there. When I started this work, we didn't have extra money to hire help and we had no relatives living near us. So, I began with actions that I could do from home without childcare. When I started visiting congressional offices, I just scooped up my child along with a lot of quiet playthings in a diaper bag and headed out to the offices. If you choose this route, there will be mishaps. But there will also likely be laughter and very humanizing moments. I've found that meetings with my kids often turned out to be memorable and positive.

This worked for me because I happened to have children who could be content looking at books and engaging in fine motor skill activities. I'm aware that this is not an option for moms whose kids have no patience for sitting quietly! In that situation, it can be really helpful to have other moms as allies. One mom can entertain little ones while the others hold the meeting. I once sat in a waiting room with an active four-year-old boy who refused to wear shoes while his mother attended a meeting with my own tweenage activists.

🕐 Story 📖 time!

Bringing my children to congressional meetings has led to moments that even my former Congresswoman smiles about years later.

My mission for the morning: sit down for a face-to-face talk with Congresswoman Jan Schakowsky about global poverty programs. My challenge: have a thoughtful, coherent conversation with my five-year-old daughter also sitting at the table.

My preschool daughter loved to draw quietly, so I stocked a shoulder bag with lots of markers and paper, and I made sure she was busily occupied before I launched into my prepared comments about global health funding. I was convincing. I was on topic. I was making intelligent points and feeling like a real lobbyist.

Then mid-speech, I noticed the Congresswoman's eyes drift beyond my face. I saw her lips begin to twitch and her eyes begin to twinkle. Oh no.

I whipped around to see that my darling in a polka-dot party dress had just finished coloring her hand a bright, glistening red.

She was just beginning to consider where she should leave a pretty red handprint. On the table? On her fancy dress? On the chair? On her mommy?

What genius thought *markers* were a good activity for a congressional office? Oh, right. Me.

I leapt up ninja-like, grabbing my daughter's wrist in alarm and asking in my calm-yet-stressed-out-Mommy voice whether anyone might direct us to a sink, please? Luckily, everyone at the table had a good laugh about it, especially the Congresswoman, who is a grandmother. Her staff even found us some pencils to replace the markers.

A post-meeting picture of Congresswoman Jan Schakowksy displaying a picture drawn with pencils while I restrain my daughter's hand.

We all took a little break to clean up and continued the meeting, which went even better after the ice had been officially broken. The story had a very positive ending, with the Congresswoman soon agreeing to write to her colleagues in support of the Global Partnership for Education. But I never, ever packed markers for a lobby meeting again.

It's Your Turn!

1. What are some barriers to advocacy that you personally face?
2. What positive message do you tell your children when they make mistakes? Look into a mirror and give that same message to yourself. Or ask someone else—maybe your child—to say those words to you now.
3. Flip through "Part III: Advocacy Made Easy" and skim the actions described there. Which action do you think would be easiest for you? Is there any reason you could not do that today?
4. Now, consider which action you think would be hardest. Why do you think that would be the most difficult action for you to take? If the very life and safety of your own child were at stake, do you think you could overcome your own barriers to do it? If you feel you can't do something because of a current lack of resources or skills, could you think of friends or organizations to help you practice a skill or provide a resource?
5. What are some steps you could take to overcome your hesitations about advocacy? Would it help to schedule a concrete time to take an action, to prepare talking points about your issue, or to enlist the help of a friend and act together?

PART III

ADVOCACY MADE EASY

THIS "HOW-TO" SECTION WILL help take the stress out of your advocacy actions. It offers plenty of lists and tips, helps you break down some common actions into simple steps, and provides sample scripts. Even when you have some experience in activism, new steps can be intimidating. My hope is that having real-life examples and clear advice can remove barriers that might hinder you from becoming a mom-advocate or from achieving your next world-changer milestone.

 **Tips and Ideas**

Tips to find your members of Congress

For any advocacy action, you will need to know the names and contact information of officials you want to influence. How do you find the contact information for your members of Congress?

1. Visit GovTrack.us or Google "Find my member of Congress" to find similar websites with information.
2. Enter your address. If you live in a zip code shared by more than one representative, you may have to use your ZIP+4 code to get the name of your representative. You can find that number from the U.S. Postal Service website (USPS.com).
3. GovTrack.us will provide names and main phone numbers in Washington D.C. for your members of Congress as well as their websites. Visit their individual sites to get contact information for their local offices, so you can call, write, and visit them there as well!

This section provides step-by-step instructions and my own commentary about the following advocacy actions, which are roughly organized in the order of time it takes to accomplish each task. Notice that I didn't say the tasks are organized based on "ease" or "effort." What is easy for one mom may be a big challenge for another!

◁ The online action
◁ The phone call

- ◁ The handwritten letter
- ◁ The letter to the editor
- ◁ The protest
- ◁ The playdate with a purpose
- ◁ The classroom project
- ◁ The town hall meeting
- ◁ The lobby meeting
- ◁ The fundraiser

Take the action that fits you in this moment. It's likely that not all of them will sync with your capability or resources right now. That's okay! Your abilities and appetite for advocacy will change over time, allowing you to stretch yourself when the time is right.

As you consider which advocacy actions are right for you, consider this study from the Congressional Management Foundation.[16] The authors wanted to know what actions make the most impact on members of Congress. A survey of congressional aides revealed that a face-to-face meeting with constituents is most likely to influence a member's actions on undecided issues. The least effective actions are generic form messages that lack any personal touch from their constituents. Other high-impact advocacy actions rank in between. Additionally, a visit from a constituent has far more influence compared to a visit from a paid lobbyist!

---

[16] Bradford Fitch, Kathy Goldschmidt, & Nicole Folk Cooper, "Citizen-Centric Advocacy: The Untapped Power of Constituent Engagement," Congressional Management Foundation, 2017.

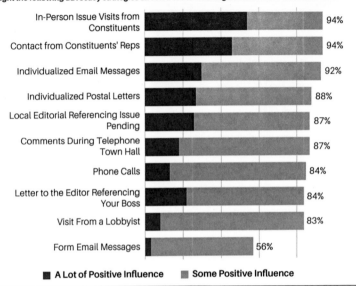

Influence of Advocacy Strategies on Undecided Member of Congress

If your Member/Senator has not already arrived at a firm decision on an issue, how much influence might the following advocacy strategies directed to the *Washington office* have on his/her decision?

In-Person Issue Visits from Constituents	94%
Contact from Constituents' Reps	94%
Individualized Email Messages	92%
Individualized Postal Letters	88%
Local Editorial Referencing Issue Pending	87%
Comments During Telephone Town Hall	87%
Phone Calls	84%
Letter to the Editor Referencing Your Boss	84%
Visit From a Lobbyist	83%
Form Email Messages	56%

■ A Lot of Positive Influence ■ Some Positive Influence

(n = 190-192)
Source: 2015 survey of congressional staff, including Chiefs of Staff, Communications Directors, Legislative Directors, and Legislative Assistants.
Published in: *Citizen-Centric Advocacy: The Untapped Power of Constituent Engagement*, Congressional Management Foundation, 2017. https://www.congressfoundation.org/citizen-centric-advocacy-2017

Building Your Advocacy Village

If you feel you can't take some actions because you lack certain skills or resources, look at it as an opportunity to do some "village building." Bring in friends or colleagues who excel in the areas where you are uncertain. An action that seems right up the alley of a friend when it's not your cup of tea is a golden opportunity to invite that friend to collaborate with you. When you offer someone the chance to help, they are likely to become more invested in your cause. They might even join your local advocacy group!

Examine your to-do list and determine which of your friends, family, or organizations might have resources to help with specific tasks? The answer might even be a public library or a house of worship. If you have a group of mom-advocates around you, you can start pooling your resources and asking specific questions like:

- Who has a car to help get to meetings?
- Who has a video conference account to help with remote group meetings or online lobby meetings with Congressional staff in D.C.?
- Who knows a responsible teenager who can play with kids while moms write letters to Congress?
- Who has the skills to proofread your letters to the editor?
- Who has a room where everyone can meet?

It might be uncomfortable to ask for help, but I find volunteers want to be useful and add value to the group. Such requests can begin to form a powerful team around you.

Notes

CHAPTER 17

THE ONLINE ACTION

WHILE YOU WILL ALWAYS hear me singing the praises of reaching out personally to aides and members of Congress, I recognize such meetings aren't ideal for everyone. What is a busy mom to do? Use online tools! Internet resources are designed to connect people to congressional offices with ease. They make a good entry point for beginning advocates.

These tools can be very useful when:

- An issue moves quickly and many advocates need to be notified immediately
- A person is so intimidated by other advocacy methods or so strapped for time that this is the only action they can take
- An organization wants to build broad awareness about an issue
- An organization wants to build up a database of people who care about the issue

Mom-of-three, Rochelle Shane from Bloomfield Township, Michigan, is a fan of online actions. She's a member of Moms-Rising, a national organization known for online tools that help folks take action on a variety of issues affecting the lives of mothers. Rochelle believes these online platforms are very valuable because they can reach a high volume of people very quickly and capture their feedback to Congress right away. "It's very effective because of how accessible it is," she says. "Regardless of where someone is, even if they are out somewhere, they are checking their social media. They can see an action right away without waiting. It's more convenient and that's what makes it so productive!"

Let's look at three common ways to advocate online and explore their pros and cons.

One-Click Online Petitions

You've probably seen petitions on your friends' social media posts. Fill in your address, click one button, and you're done. So easy! Your name and address will be added to a list of thousands of other supporters and delivered to the office of a specific person, like the president or the secretary of education.

Congressional offices are aware that these online petitions can be influenced by people using multiple email addresses, so they are not as effective as actions with a more personal touch. Still, it's a quick way to submit your opinion and an excellent way for organizations to identify allies. Once you take an online action with a group, they will have your contact information so they can encourage you to take the next step by either donating or taking a bigger action.

Web-Generated Emails

The upside of using email to contact an office is that you can comfortably type away at your keyboard. You don't have to find paper, pen, envelopes or stamps. A customized, personal email is a good way to contact your member of Congress quickly. However, it can be a problem if you don't know what to write!

That's where web-generated email campaigns come in. These websites allow you to select from various talking points and type in your own personal touches to make the email message uniquely yours. When you press "send," it will instantly deliver messages to both of your senators and your representative all at the same time.

The trick here is that it is pretty easy for offices to automatically sort out all the messages like yours and send you an automatically generated response. Your opinion does get tallied with others, but it's kind of like robots talking to each other. You might have more impact if you rewrite the sample email in your own words, hit print, and then use the regular U.S. postal system to mail your message to the local district office of your member of Congress. That ensures an actual human will have to open your letter, read it, and forward it to another human who has to respond to it. The more staff power an office has to use to respond to your request, the more they notice it. But nothing beats the internet for speed!

Online "Letter to the Editor" Tools

This is by far my favorite kind of online advocacy aid. Letters to the editor published in local papers are great because they show your members of Congress that your community is publicly talking about your issue.

Your letter will potentially be seen by thousands of people via local media and will reach even more if it is posted or shared online. In addition, you can have friends and neighbors print out your letter and mail it to your member of Congress, saying they read your letter and agree with you.

Not as many activists write these letters because it can be daunting to come up with a succinct description of your issue in less than 200 words, which is the typical word limit for most letters to the editor. But many organizations offer online tools that provide a nice template you can customize, and many allow you to send it to your paper directly from the website. How cool is that?

Just be sure to rephrase your message in your own style—don't copy the template text word for word. If more than a few people submit a letter that an editor can recognize as duplicates from a master file, you run the risk of not being published and of getting a bad reputation at your hometown newspaper.

CHAPTER 18

THE PHONE CALL

TONGUE-TIED. HEART POUNDING. I approached my phone like it was some sort of hotline to the president.

I was making my first call to my member of Congress. I'm not sure why I was so scared. I must have been afraid that someone on the other end was going to challenge my ideas or berate me for speaking up. Guess what? That never happened.

Calling Congress is not really difficult or time-consuming, once you get over being nervous. But your calls can have profound effects on public policy. Let me demystify the process of calling Congress so I can spare you the stress I once felt. You can even make the calls fun!

It's *Super* Easy

Even though I was a tad freaked out the first time I did it, these days I usually call Congress while I'm mommy multitasking: doing laundry, making lunch, whatever. It does not take your full attention or much of your time.

You Won't Be Talking to a Member of Congress

Relax! The person picking up the phone will almost certainly be a staffer who is not a specialist on your issue. The job of that person is to politely take your message, write it down, and get your name and maybe your address to ensure you're a constituent.

The staffers keep a tally of opinions from callers. You might think your phone call will be too minor to matter, but relatively few people even make the effort to call their congressional representatives, especially about topics that are not the current hot-button news. So, even ten phone calls on the same issue on the same day can be very significant.

Help Is Available

Most advocacy organizations will supply talking points and information you can refer to during your call. In fact, most will provide a sample script that you can customize to make it personal.

You Can Use Notes

Pssst. You're on a phone. They can't see you! Here's a slightly embarrassing confession: I write my name at the top of my paper. Yes. When I make a call, I am literally reading my own name. I figure if I stumble over my own name, the rest of the call probably won't go so well. But the person on the other end of the phone can't see that

I'm reading my name or any other notes. In this situation, using a cheat sheet is not cheating.

Calling Can Be More Fun with Friends

Remember I said even ten calls together can make a difference? Have a little call-in party. Each call only lasts two minutes, so you could fit in five calls on a short coffee break. Heck, if there is a line at Starbucks, you might have ten calls completed by the time the barista hands you your latte!

Story time!

I held an impromptu call-in party with friends at my local pool on a hot summer day that got an unexpectedly immediate response. My RESULTS group had been trying for weeks to get a response from a senator's aide without success. So, one morning, I walked around the pool with my cell phone and asked my sunbathing mom-friends to call in and use a two-sentence script while we watched our mini-swimmers. By the time I got to the other side of the pool, the aide called me back and said, "Okay, okay! We can talk. You can stop the call-in!"

Mission accomplished.

Sample Script

To make it even easier, I'll give you a sample of a bare-bones call-in script. This script relates to global education, but you can take the basic idea and modify it for your issue. You can add flowery language and details about the issue to extend it by another twenty or thirty seconds, but this script will get you started.

Aide: Hello. Congresswoman Bush's office.

Me: Hi, I'm Cynthia Changyit Levin, a constituent, with a message for the Congresswoman.

Aide: Go ahead, please.

Me: I'd like her to support H. Res. 225 about the Global Partnership for Education. It affirms America's role in improving access to quality inclusive public education for children in the most impoverished nations.

Aide: Thank you, may I have your zip code?

Me: 63104.

Aide: Thank you. Have a good day.

Me: Thank you. You, too.

Ta-dah! Not so bad, is it?

The most important parts of the call are the bill number (if your issue has one) and your zip code to let the office know you are a constituent. Compose your own message or find a script from an advocacy organization you trust. Next, pick up the phone and dial!

Now give it a try! Here's a form to get you started. Just fill in the blanks and you'll be ready to make your call. Remember, it's not cheating to read right off of your paper.

 Tips and Ideas

Tip for a quick confidence boost

When everything else in my day is spinning out of control, I find it empowering to make a phone call to Congress. I can hang up the phone after leaving my ten-second message and think, "There. I did that. I helped." Other things might still go wrong, but after I've made that call, no one can take that feeling away from me.

Phone Call "Cheat Sheet"

Hello! My name is (*your name*) _____.

I'm a constituent living in (*your city*) _____ **and I'd like to**

leave a message for (*Senator/Representative*_____).

I'm concerned about . . .
(*Give a one sentence description of your concern*)

I would like the (*Senator/Representative*_____) **to . . .**
(*Give a clear, one sentence description of the action you'd like them to take, including any bill names or number designations if there is a specific piece of legislation you want them to support or oppose*)

Do you need my address or zip code?
(*Provide if necessary*)

Thank you for taking my comment. Have a nice day!
(*GREAT JOB! Now, do a little dance and have a tasty snack. You deserve it!*)

Notes

CHAPTER 19

THE HANDWRITTEN LETTER

WHEN I ENCOURAGE NEW advocates—young or old—to handwrite letters to Congress, they always ask, "Do we *really* have to write them by hand?" My answer is: *yes!*

I know that our digital age makes handwriting seem quaint, but unless you have a condition that makes it difficult for you to write, you should hand write your letter to Congress for two reasons.

1. It sets your message apart from the masses of spam emails and tweets hurled at Congress every hour. Handwriting letters is becoming a bit of a lost art. Like handwriting thank-you notes, hardly anyone ever does it anymore. So, when an office gets your handwritten letter, it will be more memorable.
2. It shows you are authentic. Handwriting proves you didn't digitally copy and paste someone else's message. Even if you

A young constituent used different colored markers to make her letter a work of art as well!

do hand copy a letter word for word, you have to take the time to look at each word and write it out with purposeful intention. The author of a handwritten letter did not blindly cut and paste something into a message without even reading it.

So, hooray for handwriting!

Writing Effective Letters

To write an effective letter to Congress, you should:

1. Keep it short and personal
2. Utilize the EPIC format to ensure you stay focused
3. Present a clear request
4. Sign the letter with your name, title, and address

1. Keep It Short and Personal

The most effective letters share something personal about a constituent. Write about your experiences and why you care about the issue you want your member of Congress to address. Are you afraid you haven't personally experienced a hardship worth describing? That's okay. Describe a news story you heard or read and how the story made you feel. That kind of anecdote even helps illustrate that your issue is important enough to be in the media! Your letter should not be longer than one page. Staying brief will help keep you focused and to the point.

2. Use EPIC Format

I know it's hard to detail complicated human feelings in one page. Whether I'm starting a letter from scratch or tweaking a template, I like to use the tried and true "EPIC" format I learned from RESULTS organizers. EPIC stands for Engage, Problem, Inform, Call to Action, and it helps me get my scattered mommy-brain thoughts in order so I can create a clear, effective, one-page handwritten letter.

- **Engage.** Engage the reader's attention. You could use a question, a personal experience, startling statement, or even a thank-you to your member of Congress for an action you appreciated. Describing a personal connection to an issue can be a powerful beginning.
- **Problem.** Briefly state the problem you want your reader to address. I often add statistics in this section.

↲ **Inform.** Inform the reader of a solution or illustrate how the solution can help.

↲ **Call to action.** *Clearly* state what you want your reader to do. Your call to action will be most effective if you can frame it in the form of a yes-or-no question.

Just one or two sentences in each section will do the trick! Here is an example of the body of an EPIC letter about low-income housing. The sections are labeled to illustrate the different categories.

Dear Senator,

(Engage) America is in a housing crisis. I recently helped a friend in poverty rent an apartment so her family could live in a safe community, and I learned how difficult this is for many Missourians.

(Problem) Millions of low-income working families struggle just to put a roof over their heads. Since 1960, renters' median earnings have gone up five percent while rents have risen by sixty-one percent.

(Inform) One way to address this problem is to shift tax resources to support a "Renters Tax Credit" for low- and moderate-income renters. This would give taxpayers a credit equal to any amount in rent that they pay over thirty percent of their income.

(Call to Action) Will you please support a renter's tax credit and prioritize low-income working families in the upcoming revisions to housing and tax policies?

3. Present a Clear Request

Make it crystal clear what action you want your member of Congress to take. It's best if you have a bill number and the official name of a bill, but even if you don't have that information, make your request for action so clear that you can put your request in the form of a "yes or no" question. It could be something like "Will you help save the lives of moms and kids around the world by signing the Reach Every Mother and Child Act?" I underline or use a bright highlighter on my request sentence, so the reader can't possibly miss it.

4. Don't Forget to Sign

If you have an illegible signature like I do, it's important to print your name along with your address. Your address lets the office know that you live in their district and it's their job to represent you. Write your address both on the return address area of your outside envelope *and* on the inside letter itself. Busy office staffers move quickly, and your envelope may get separated from your letter. At best, you might not receive a response to your request. At worst, your letter might be thrown away if another staffer sees no proof that you're a constituent and a potential voter.

Using a title is optional, but feel free to use one. As silly as it might seem to stay-at-home moms like me who always feel like an unpaid mash-up of "Chef/Maid/Private Math Tutor/Psychologist/Head Zookeeper," a title can signal to your member that you have a place in your community and you probably influence others who vote in their district.

Titles aren't as hard to come by as you might think, even if you don't have a professional position. Do you sit on any volunteer committees? Are you a member of a religious community? Are you a Scout leader or a youth sports coach?

Guess what? Even if you are just using talking points about global poverty from the ONE Campaign website, you're doing unpaid work for them and that makes you an official ONE volunteer. Flaunt that title, baby.

Don't Overthink It!

A letter to Congress shouldn't take you more than five minutes to write. I've coached new folks who agonized over a letter for over thirty minutes, eventually taking it home for more tweaking. I wonder if they ever sent the letter at all.

"Please help kids in the world be healthy," from a child can be memorable.

Here's the truth: perfection isn't necessary. A hastily written message with poor handwriting is more effective than a master-piece that never gets mailed. Think like a child. I've included a picture of a letter my preschooler wrote about global health. It says simply, "Please help kids in the world be healthy." Her letter got a response, just like mine did, and it helped us pass global child health legislation (okay, she also wrote "I love yoo," so maybe that's what made it so effective!).

 Tips and Ideas

Tips to get your letter delivered faster

Letters mailed to your local district offices arrive much faster than the ones mailed to Washington, D.C. If you mail your letter all the way to Capitol Hill, it will take more travel time, plus it will be held for another couple of weeks to get through anthrax bacteria screening.

Younger readers may not recall the anthrax bioterrorism attacks of 2001, which involved media outlets, U.S. Senate offices, and the State Department. Sadly, five people died and many people—including thirty-one Capitol Hill staffers—tested positive for anthrax.

However, local offices still receive mail without screening. Local aides log your opinion and then forward your letter to their D.C. office. I once had a Congresswoman who carried her own constitu-ent letters back to D.C. every week in her own briefcase!

Write Often and Ask Others to Join You

Ideally, letter writing is combined with other forms of advocacy, and frequent letters will bolster the case of anyone arriving in a congressional office to speak about an issue in person. Even so, it usually takes many letters to inspire a member of Congress to take action.

So enlist neighbors, spouses, children, Scouting troops, book clubs, and anyone you know to write letters with you. As a Bread for the World organizer for my church, I've collected and delivered hundreds of letters at a time from my congregation. That kind of citizen advocacy really makes senators and representatives sit up and take notice.

What happens after they receive your letter? Well, most of the time you'll get a form letter in response, although my children have occasionally received personal letters from senators and representatives over the years. But don't let a form letter response discourage you. You never know how far up the office chain your letter will go!

CHAPTER 20

THE LETTER TO THE EDITOR

A LETTER TO THE editor is a very short letter written by a reader and printed in the opinion section of a newspaper. It certainly takes a bit more work to be published in a professional newspaper than to post an opinion on your personal social media platform. Why make the time and effort to write one?

1. **To inform others in your community about your issue.** Your local newspaper gets delivered directly to many more people than most can reach by hosting informational events.
2. **To attract the attention of members of Congress.** Congressional staff check the media every day to see what constituents in the community are saying about their bosses as a way for them to see what potential voters are talking about.

3. **To engage other activists.** Others can share it on social media, print it out, and mail it to members of Congress. They can even write their own supportive letters to the editor in response to yours!

Using methods I learned from RESULTS, I found that writing a letter to the editor isn't very different from writing a personal letter to Congress. But you must follow rules determined by the newspaper, which can generally be found in the opinion sections of a newspaper's print edition and website.

Small papers may publish every letter that meets their standards; larger papers publish only a small fraction of the letters they receive. Follow the strategies below to boost your chances of getting published and to make your letters more effective.

Grab Attention with a Current Event

People have pretty short attention spans, so your first line should be highly engaging. Can you think of an interesting angle that hooks the reader in to read more? Connecting to a recent national or local event always helps.

One of the easiest hooks to use is a reference to an article the newspaper has published previously. For instance, when a newspaper reported that a traveling college student was diagnosed on a Missouri campus with tuberculosis (TB), I used that local angle to talk about TB as a global problem that needs American financial support.

You will increase your odds of being chosen if you write a response to an article or someone else's letter to the editor published within the last seven days. Include the name of the piece and the date it was published in the first line of your letter. If you submit via email, make it obvious in your subject line that your letter is in reaction to a major event or in response to an article the newspaper printed. For example, your subject line could be: "Response to 'America Should Act Now to End Global Disease' printed 4/1."

Use EPIC Format

You can construct your letter using the "EPIC" format described in the previous section about writing letters to Congress. Remember to **E**ngage the listener, state the **P**roblem, **I**nform about a solution, and give a **C**all to action. All you really need is one line for each section. Of course, you don't have to adhere strictly to this format, but it can help you get started.

Be Concise and Precise

Most papers prefer to print letters between 150-200 words. Some will enforce a word limit very strictly and will not consider letters over a certain word count. The phrase "less is more" definitely applies. The editor of my local newspaper, the *St. Louis Post-Dispatch*, shared that limits of physical space on the opinion page mean that editors prefer short, focused letters. Stick to one subject and stay on topic without rambling.

Correct grammar will also help your chances of being published. Have a friend proofread it if you can. Reading it out loud to myself helps me catch missing words that might unintentionally change the meaning of the whole piece!

Connect to Your Community

Help your readers understand why your issue matters to your community. That is ultimately what your members of Congress want to know, and they are the decision-makers. What experiences do readers have in common with people you seek to help? You could use the angle of summer vacation to explain how nutrition programs are necessary when many kids go hungry without school lunch. Sadly, most states have no shortage of articles about gun violence to relate to the safety of children and parents.

Challenge without Attack

It's healthy and engaging to question elected officials. Challenging the status quo is what an activist does. However, I recommend avoiding personal attacks. They are not respectful and rarely persuasive. Also, if you are writing as a volunteer for a nonpartisan organization, be careful not to damage its reputation by making remarks that maliciously criticize a particular political party, candidate, or civic leader.

Call Others to Action

End your letter by asking for specific action from your members of Congress. Mentioning their names increases the likelihood that they will see your letter because many congressional offices do daily internet searches by name. Make a clear request that leaves no room to doubt what action you want them to take. If you have a number for a bill or resolution, like "House Resolution 189," be sure and include it. Show them your passion for the issue and ask them to make a difference. You can also invite readers into action by asking them to call or write.

Pay Attention to the Details

Include your name, address, email, and a daytime and evening phone number with your submission to the paper. The newspaper won't publish this information, but they might use it to contact you and confirm that you are the author. And be sure to check the Letters to the Editor page of your newspaper or its website for guidelines on submitting a letter. Some prefer emails; others require you to upload your words through an online form; others accept physical, mailed copies. Follow all instructions closely to give your letter the best chance for publication.

Write with Others

If you have an advocacy group, send in several letters to the editor from different volunteers. Each person will bring their own distinctive writing style to the exercise. Having a choice of letters allows the editor to pick one that best fits the readership.

Whether the paper prints your letters or not, a group effort demonstrates that more than one person in the community cares about a particular cause. This could influence editors to run more articles and opinion pieces about that issue.

Story time!

Working together in a group can make writing letters to the editor more fun and less stressful. When I wrote my first letter, I was alone and rather nervous. I wish I had enjoyed some in-person support as I clicked the "submit" button. A year later, I gathered four of my friends—all moms—to write to our little newspaper together.

The paper had just printed my 700-word opinion piece about the $5 billion shortfall the Global Fund to AIDS, TB and Malaria would soon face because donor nations were backing out of their promises. My friends wrote letters responding to my writing. I was amazed how different people took the same information and talking points and expressed it in completely different ways!

Joan was concerned with the moral aspects of the issue. Her tone was strong, patriotic, and proud. She placed her personal commitment firmly in her call to action line by declaring, "I have written to my members of Congress" and urging readers to do the same.

Kerry attacked the exercise with the enthusiasm of her sons playing soccer. As a teacher, she has a great appreciation for language. She immediately knocked out 192 words comparing the needed funding ($1 billion in 2009) to the amount of Christmas bonuses given to Merrill Lynch executives after the Wall Street bailout that year ($3.6 billion). Her statement was intellectual, shocking, and timely. She viewed the constraint to edit her letter down to 150 words as a fun puzzle.

Sonja, a practical and giving soul, saw the brilliant and simple opportunity to offer readers different ways to help. She invited them to help the Global Fund by writing members of Congress, making direct individual contributions and even using a special Starbucks card branded for an AIDS organization that was available in stores that year.

Eriko chose to acknowledge our community's global outlook and legacy of caring. She acknowledged the local need of neighbors living in poverty and urged readers to remember that we are all one people in a vast human family around the world. It totally aligned with the way she parented in a trilingual home honoring her daughter's Japanese and Malaysian heritage.

In the end, our local papers published the letters by Kerry and Eriko. Because of space constraints, not every letter could be printed. Yet four letters coming in at the same time about the same topic swayed the editor to pick from them to represent all the submissions.

Writing together as a group was eye-opening for me and made me feel more excited about my own writing. I could see more possibilities inspired by the energy and life experiences of my friends. They taught me the lesson that I was trying to teach them: there are limitless ways to write these letters!

"Write Letters, Send Them In"

Hands down, this is my favorite piece of advice from my media hero, RESULTS volunteer Willie Dickerson, who estimates he's been published over 1,000 times. He gets more media printed than any volunteer I've ever heard about, and he should! He has written at least one letter every single day for years.

When he says, "Write letters, send them in," he points out that a draft languishing on your computer won't be seen by an editor. Further, he's fond of reminding writers that one hundred percent of the letters we never submit will never get published. Don't agonize over it so long that your hook goes stale or you lose courage.

These days, even as an experienced letter-writer, I usually have to write five or ten letters to different newspapers to get one published. So, just keep writing and send 'em in!

Notes

CHAPTER 21

THE PROTEST

WHEN A BIG MOMENT comes around, protests can be a powerful way for a local community to weigh in together or for massive groups to congregate in a high-profile destination like Washington, D.C. There are times when many individuals uniting together can attract attention and stimulate needed actions.

Protests can be a powerful tool to harness the negative emotions of a moment and inspire positive, long-lasting change. They can persuade leaders to change a course of action or even energize citizens into voting an elected official out of office.

As parents, we need to decide whether it is appropriate to involve our children in protest activities. We must recognize that these experiences are not set up to be learning exercises for the benefit of our children. Large crowds, uncomfortable temperatures, and heightened emotions can create difficult situations for both adults and children. Yet some issues demand our presence, despite the challenging circumstances. There may come a day when you feel it is important for your child to also be present at a protest or when your teen demands to be included.

Unlike advocacy actions taken privately at home, public protesting might involve tear gas, gunfire, or other physical threats. Your safety and the safety of your children should be paramount when you consider joining a public protest event. Emotions can run hot in large crowds and what starts as a peaceful protest can descend into chaos and violence. Before you join a protest, carefully consider who will be protesting what, where the event will be held, and how high emotions are running in your area.

Some issues have more potential for violence than others. Protests and rallies against gun violence sometimes draw out armed counter-protesters. Marches against police violence can inspire higher tensions between police and activists.

Also consider the format of the event, which can range from rallies and vigils that stay in one place to marches that cover miles of territory. Is it better for your family to be in a march where you can duck easily out of the route or at a rally where small kids can sit on a blanket far from the center of the action? You decide what is best for your particular family situation.

I recommend choosing an environment that allows you to be the most present to your children and provides the best possible chances for peaceful gatherings.

Before a Protest

Here are some tips for choosing and preparing to attend a protest event with children.

- Look for an event during daylight hours for better visibility, greater probability of peaceful action, and less grumpy children.
- Choose an event at a location that will allow you to leave early, with the least amount of trouble, if your child gets tired or has an urgent need for a bathroom.
- Discuss the issue with your kids days ahead of time to help them understand the issue and give them time to ask questions.
- Help kids make their own signs. Thinking about what they want on their signs and how they want to express it can be part of their learning experience.
- Discuss the tone of the march with your kids. The March for Science had a serious message about climate change and other issues, but marchers mostly came with a light-hearted attitude. Black Lives Matter protests often had an urgent air of life-and-death matters, and it was important for older kids to know they would be standing in solidarity with survivors of traumatic experiences.

At the Protest

Here are tips for taking kids to protests that have been gleaned from experienced parent protesters.

For Everyone
- Pack water.
- Prepare for the weather: hats and sunscreen in the summer, ponchos for rain, or warm gloves and other outerwear for early spring and winter.
- Wear good, comfortable shoes.

- Stay close to each other.
- Bring a bandana for each person, which can be useful for wiping a sweaty face with cool water or protecting from tear gas.

For Young Children

- Dress kids in clothes with pockets and make sure important information is in the pockets. Very important info like allergies and parent phone numbers could even be written on arms or on a keychain safety-pinned to the child's clothes.
- Bring one lightweight sign for every two to three marchers so all can take turns when tykes tire of carrying the sign.
- Attend with another family with kids for fewer complaints of boredom.
- Snacks, snacks, snacks.

For Older Kids

- Agree to rules before you arrive. For instance, "Don't go into the thick of the crowd." Or "Be respectful and positive."
- Charge all cell phones and conserve battery charge for communication with each other.
- Carry ID.
- Don't wear contact lenses in case of tear gas.
- Have a designated meeting space a few blocks from the protest in case you get separated.
- Choose a spot where you can hear the speeches, if possible, so your kids can learn.
- For sensitive human rights issues like Black Lives Matter, discuss what it means to be a good ally if you are not a person of color. For example, counsel white kids to follow Black leadership and not start chants on their own. Also, taking and posting smiling selfies when marching next to people in pain is in poor taste no matter how many people around you are doing it.

↵ Discuss how to behave if yelled at, harassed, threatened, or arrested or if they see it happen to someone else.

↵ For sensitive issues, tell your kids not to post pictures of local organizers or other protesters on social media because that might lead them to be targeted by extremists.

Yes, those last two points are alarming. And that's why you must give serious consideration to your family's safety before showing up for a protest event. Not all marches are simply a walk in the park.

I'll say it again: Protests are not set up to be learning exercises for the benefit of our children.

⏱ Story 📖 time!

Ilina Ewan of Raleigh, North Carolina, has been protesting about a wide range of issues with her two boys since 2010. In those days, she and her husband used to supply them with snacks and take them in strollers. As teenagers, her sons marched with her through the 2016 Women's March, the 2018 March for Our Lives, and some 2020 Black Lives Matter protests.

Ilina believes strongly in the power of protests to pump energy into a movement to jumpstart action. She thinks a critical piece of successful protesting is for organizers to provide a call to action that will keep protesters engaged long after the marching is done.

"A lot of people think a protest is a lot of loudmouths out there having their say and it doesn't do anything. But I think that it actually does help draw attention to an issue," Ilina said. "The key piece of a protest is to have a call to action in your back pocket. If you protest for protesting's sake, that does not necessarily get you effective attention. Or it gets you short-term attention. But you can have a list for protesters that says, 'Here's what we want to see happen, and here's where you need to help us.' That's the piece that's often missing."

Protests can be a memorable time that brings a group together for inspiration. Ilina elaborated, "You always have that moment to go back to, to say, 'Do you remember that time hundreds of people showed up outside of Senator Thom Tillis' office to talk about refugees and immigration?' It gives you a frame of reference and a good visual. Then, you go from there as a catapult toward what you want to change.

"It's one thing to get enough people to galvanize around an issue for an event. It's another to keep them engaged to build momentum. It doesn't stop with a protest. It's a step in generating more change."

Meredith Dodson of Washington, D.C. admits that frequent exposure to protests has inspired her two children to utilize some interesting tactics to advocate for their own personal causes, like increased screen time, at home.
Photo credit: Meredith Dodson.

CHAPTER 22

THE PLAYDATE WITH A PURPOSE

HERE'S AN ADVOCACY ACTION with something familiar at its core: a playdate! Some people call this a "Playdate with a Purpose." When I gathered a group of local moms, we called it "Social Justice for Social Moms." This formula worked very well when our children were babies and toddlers.

Where did I find these moms? Mostly we connected as we circulated around the neighborhood. Obvious visual cues like baby carriers and strollers signaled that we were in a similar stage of life. Even if being a mom was all we had in common, that was often enough of a draw for first-time moms to get together. We enjoyed hanging out to make friends and ponder new thoughts.

Purposeful Playdate Guidelines

1. Set aside two hours a month for the gathering. Arrange for someone to entertain the kids in a different room.
2. Allow at least half an hour for snacking, chatting, and settling stray toddlers who will want to know what's going on in the Mommy Room.
3. Educate the group about a social justice issue. A short video or a clip from a movie can be very powerful. If you don't have one available, the group could read aloud from a news article or a book.
4. Dedicate the final half-hour to call or write appropriate elected officials with a request for specific action.

When I started our group, none of us were committed to a particular cause. We used our meetings to learn new things and process potentially upsetting information as a group. Our topics ranged from global education to waste reduction in our homes to recruitment of child soldiers in the Democratic Republic of Congo to hunger in America to global access to immunizations.

I treasured how I got to know the women of my community better by their choice of issues and their insights in discussions. Looking back at that time, my friend Kerry reflected, "When you're on a personal journey, it's really nice to have company."

In my opinion, these meetings are more appealing than the ever-popular book clubs because no one has to feel shame about falling behind in the reading. You show up, learn together, discuss real-world topics, and take action. Nothing in that formula involves homework stress, and all of it leads to feeling more informed and empowered!

Tips and Ideas

Tips to sharing the organizing load in your group

- Alternate which mom watches the kids or share the cost of a sitter
- Rotate the job of hosting
- Vary the issue and who picks it
- Invite everyone to bring snacks to share

Be mindful that not everyone in the group may have similar economic resources or hosting abilities. Find tactful solutions with creativity and kindness to help everyone participate if you have members of your group who are unhoused, don't have a car, or experience a financial burden in providing food or sitter fees. We never want to perpetuate injustices within a social justice group!

Understand that not everyone in your social circle will want to join your activism exploration. Don't be upset if some of your friends choose to sit out. Advocacy isn't for everyone. Like me, you might only have a handful of friends who want to join initially. But a little group can plant seeds that will grow, especially if you're all having fun and talking about your events in a positive way that is inclusive of new parents.

As cultural anthropologist Margaret Mead once said, "Never doubt that a small group of thoughtful, committed citizens can change the world; indeed, it's the only thing that ever has."

Notes

CHAPTER 23

THE CLASSROOM PROJECT

YOUR CHILD'S CLASSROOM OR Scout troop can provide the perfect opportunity to pursue your desire to advocate while also involving your kids. At the same time, it gives you a chance to work with your child's teacher or Scout leader and to spend some time with your kid's friends.

Classroom Opportunities

I like to partner with teachers for two reasons. First, I like helping children understand they are connected to decisions made about them and other children in the world. Second, I like to have a good relationship with my kids' teachers. Several teachers I've met— from preschool to high school—have been receptive to a respectful offer to help build a classroom advocacy project into their existing curriculum. Obviously, these projects will vary depending on the age of the students and the amount of time you have to complete it. Here are some examples for different age groups.

Preschool and Kindergarten

Storytime is a natural place for a mom to fit into a classroom when the kids are too young to read on their own. For two-year-olds, volunteer to read a story about the universal nature of love around the world. I like Mem Fox's *Whoever You Are*.

As kids are able to understand more involved stories, ask to read true-story books that respectfully illustrate cultural differences and offer solutions to poverty. Good choices include *Beatrice's Goat* by Page McBrier, about a girl who can go to school only because her family can sell goat milk, or *One Hen* by Katie Smith Milway, which shows how microfinance helps a boy buy chickens, fund

A picture of me reading *Whoever You Are* to a group of children in Morton Grove, IL.

his own education, and eventually run a successful business. You might have to change complicated wording or condense the stories for time, but young nonreaders rarely mind such edits (unless they are trying to draw out a bedtime story).

Drawing pictures of the story is a great way to help the children process what they just heard.

Elementary School

If your child's classroom teacher is interested in your issue or is teaching persuasive writing, then you might have a great ally for an advocacy project. When kids are able to write full paragraphs, they are just as ready as an adult to write a letter to Congress.

An elementary-school-sized advocacy project can be a great way to combine lessons on reading, writing, and cultural studies. Work with the teacher to provide current background information about the problem you want to address, decide how extensive the project will be, determine a schedule, and specify who will be responsible for which elements.

Youth-centered fiction books such as *A Long Walk to Water* by Linda Sue Park can provide a great centering point for an advocacy activity. Park's story tells of two Sudanese eleven-year-olds in 1985 and 2008 and helps young readers connect emotionally to the problems children face when they have no access to clean water. After the class has read the story, you can explain how all of us—including kids—should work together to solve problems like access to water. Show them how writing letters to Congress can be a good place to start.

How do you teach kids to write letters to Congress? The same way you teach adults! The EPIC format mentioned in the previous letter-writing section is easy enough for kids to use as long as you give them guidance and freedom to come up with their own talking points. I like to write all the kids' ideas on the board in front of the room. It helps validate their thinking and makes it easy for them to pick the ones that they like for their personal letters.

Kids are generally more willing than adults to write letters on the spot and even read them out loud to each other. Some teachers I've worked with are happy to create a classroom assignment to write letters, which are graded for grammar and punctuation. Sending the letters to Congress should be optional. Remember that your role is to teach a citizenship skill. The decision to exercise that skill should be up to them. Requiring a student to take a political action could have negative consequences for you, the teacher, and the school.

Tips and Ideas

Tips for creating a successful elementary school project

- Choose a nonpartisan issue, like hunger, that kids can relate to.
- Focus on the positive parts of citizen engagement.
- If you write letters to Congress, make it clear that the students are not required to mail the letters. Give them the information they need, such as the mailing address. You can even practice formatting the envelope since many kids don't know how to do this. But allow the kids to decide whether to add the stamp and mail the letter.

⏱ Story 📖 time!

Cooperating with my daughter's reading teacher led to a school field trip I could not have accomplished on my own. Mrs. Schmidt used *A Long Walk to Water* by Linda Sue Park to introduce fourth- and fifth-grade students to challenges kids face in Sudan. Reading the book and watching supporting videos prepared the students intellectually and emotionally.

All of the kids experimented with the best way to carry water for a long distance.

My portion of the program explored the question: "What can *we* do to help people have water?" We created a walking field trip to the nearby library to fill up empty water jugs and carry them back so students could physically feel what it is like to carry water. At the library, they learned about how U.S. aid helps people in developing nations gain access to clean water. We also learned how to write letters to Congress to help that happen.

After writing their letters, we filled the kids' empty water jugs and began the twenty-minute trek back to school. After school, I drove to the local congressional office with my daughters to deliver the letters. Happily, their representative, Congresswoman Jan Schakowsky, agreed to their request to sign onto the Water for the World Act!

There is a ton of room for creativity in classroom projects. Your choice of action with kids will be influenced by the abilities of the children, the willingness of the teacher, and what resources you have available. A classroom project is often unique and memorable for everyone involved.

Scout Projects

Scout projects are very similar to school projects in that you must carefully plan an age-appropriate way to present your issue and advocacy action. Many Scout leaders will be quite receptive to parent-led activities because they are usually busy parent volunteers looking for ways to help their group earn badges. They will typically welcome you with open arms if you suggest a way for the troop to earn a citizenship badge that requires no extra leader effort.

Be prepared to be very engaging with an interactive lesson for Scouts. These meetings usually happen after school, so you might be working with tired, hungry, and squirrelly children who know your activity is not required for a grade. I highly recommend activities that involve creativity and art.

I led one meeting for first-grade Girl Scout Daisies that served *five* purposes:

1. **Team building.** An art project to make a poster for their congresswoman helped the Scouts express themselves as a team.
2. **Education.** The lesson taught them basic facts about poverty and how our government works.
3. **Citizenship skills.** The group communicated with their congressional representative about a current campaign.

A Morton Grove, Illinois, Girl Scout Daisy troop decorates a poster with their "Thinking Day" message about global education.

4. **Community.** Involving the troop and their parents in the project helped build relationships and make more people aware of the issue.
5. **Public awareness.** The girls' poster hung in their Congresswoman's district office for at least three years.

You never know how far this kind of activity could lead. One of the girls I helped in middle school was awarded a $5,000 scholarship in high school for earning her Girl Scout Gold Award with an advocacy project!

CHAPTER 24

THE TOWN HALL MEETING

A TOWN HALL MEETING is an event hosted by an elected official, a congressional aide, or a candidate that is typically held at a public space so attendees can ask questions. These meetings might go by different names, such as Kitchen Table Talk or Constituent Coffee, but you can generally describe any gathering that allows the public to be active participants as a town hall meeting.

Mom-advocates can find these meetings to be very useful, especially if you have difficulty scheduling a meeting with your elected official. Advocating at town hall meetings is like a two-for-one deal because you will make yourself visible not only to your member of Congress but also to your community. A well-timed, thoughtful question will allow you to enhance your public reputation and may attract media attention. Plus, your member of Congress will be giving you an answer on the record in front of the public and possibly the media!

Most town halls I've attended are not very exciting at all. Yet these meetings allow ordinary citizens to hold their elected officials accountable for actions in D.C. This is democracy at its rawest—although not necessarily finest—form.

Make the Most of a Town Hall

Be on the lookout for any town halls scheduled near you. Some congressional representatives will list upcoming town halls on official websites. Some will publicize them on a mailing list, so be sure to sign up for your representatives' email or mail updates. Some hold town halls weekly in Washington, D.C., if you are lucky enough to be able to travel there. Sadly, others don't hold any at all.

The format for asking questions can vary from meeting to meeting. Questioners might be instructed to line up at microphones, raise their hands, or write down questions to be drawn at random from a bucket. I attended one where fewer than twenty people showed up, so an aide asked each person to state their concern in two minutes or less and responded to each participant personally.

 Tips and Ideas

Tips for taking children to a town hall meeting

If your children easily sit through a religious service without causing a disturbance, they can probably handle a typical town hall. I still encourage you to consider the time of day, what the venue will be like, and if any controversial adult topics are likely to be shouted about. I did not take my kids to a standing-room-only evening town hall after the controversial Affordable Health Care Act was passed and grown-ups were not acting like civil adults.

If I'm reasonably certain the town hall will last an hour or less and everyone will behave civilly, I enjoy bringing my kids. A bag full of quiet, no-mess activities is always a good idea if your kids are young. I recommend offering your children lollipops just as the meeting starts, which keep their mouths quietly busy without much mess.

How to Ask a Question at a Town Hall

- **Talk to someone who has attended a town hall with that member of Congress before.** Find out what the format will be and learn about their experiences with your particular member of Congress. Or ask an aide to predict how the meeting will go.

- **Invite friends/allies to help.** An ally is important if you need an interpreter to speak for you or just a tall person who can raise their hand up very high! If you have a friend willing to also ask a question, you may want to sit separately in a big audience and try a "bird-dogging" strategy: having different people ask a similar question in a different way if the speaker tries to evade the issue.

- **Show up early.** This will allow you to find a seat near the front and might even give you a chance to connect with your elected official in a relaxed manner. I once arrived early and found myself parking next to Congresswoman Jan Schakowsky. As we walked from our cars to the door, we got to chat one-on-one without other people clamoring for her attention.

- **Sit up front and wear a t-shirt with the logo of your organization.** You want to be noticed and remembered. You might even show up in newspaper pictures the next day, and your t-shirt will remind everyone of your issue.

- ↩ **Write out brief remarks that end with a clear "yes or no" question.** There's nothing wrong with reading from a paper if you are nervous.

- ↩ **Raise your hand right away if that is the format for choosing questions.** Be "first, fast, and high" and keep it up there!

- ↩ **Be brief and polite.** No one wants to listen to a meandering question, and no one wants to be insulted.

- ↩ **Share something personal about yourself.** Briefly tell everyone why you personally care about your issue, so other people can see themselves in your place. For instance, "I am a mother of young children who cares deeply about their health. When I found out that 1.5 million children per year—one every twenty seconds—die in developing countries because of a lack of vaccines, I was horrified."

- ↩ **Focus on the story more than statistics.** People are more likely to remember a touching story rather than a bunch of numbers. For example, after I mentioned the statistics about how many children die without vaccines, my dad-advocate colleague, Bob McMullen, used his turn to tell a story about a woman who personally vaccinated thousands of children. He concluded, "She just needs our help to get the vaccines!" If reporters are present, they might ask you to repeat your story for their audiences.

- ↩ **Address the audience as much as you address the member of Congress.** If possible, make eye contact with some of the audience as well as your representative. You could find like-minded people in the audience who want to join your group. Or you might educate someone who thought they were opposed to your point of view.

- **Use your loud speaking voice.** You want everyone to clearly hear about your issue and the name of your organization. Speak the truth even if your voice shakes.
- **Bring a fact sheet.** You'll usually be allowed to hand the speaker some facts about your issue and your request. That makes it efficient for them to give to the appropriate office aide to simply say, "Follow up on this!" instead of trying to remember what you said in the moment.

🕐 📖 Story time!

My favorite town hall was a constituent coffee I attended with my family on Capitol Hill when my daughters were six and eight. My husband and I arrived early at the event hosted by our Illinois senators, Dick Durbin and Mark Kirk. The girls carried dozens of hand-drawn pictures and letters from their friends asking the senators to support global vaccine programs.

Arriving separately, both senators scanned the milling crowd and made a beeline to talk to the cute little girls in the audience. They were surprised to meet the tiniest lobbyists in the room!

When the formal meeting began, I was impressed by how friendly the senators were with each other, even though Senator Durbin was a high-ranking Democrat and Senator Kirk was a seasoned Republican. This relationship wasn't like the mean-spirited TV performances I was accustomed to seeing. These were two guys with different opinions on some things and who agreed on a lot of other things.

When they opened up for questions, my hand was the first in the air! I delivered a few sentences about how we can help impoverished people who are dying from tuberculosis and HIV/AIDS and then asked the senators to allocate $1.65 billion for the Global Fund to

Fight AIDS, TB, and Malaria. The audience registered surprise at the price tag of my request, but the senators didn't miss a beat. Both served on the Subcommittee on State and Foreign Operations and were used to dealing with big numbers when deciding how to spend foreign aid dollars.

Each of them expressed admiration for the life-saving work of the Global Fund. Being savvy politicians, they didn't make promises to grant my specific number, but my message had been delivered and received in front of about fifty other constituents who heard the senators support poverty-focused foreign aid.

Afterward, my family got a photo taken with the senators that is still framed in our home. We called that picture a "double rainbow" because it's quite rare to get two senators in a picture at the same time!

My daughters in Washington, D.C., presenting Senator Dick Durbin and Senator Mark Kirk with letters and artwork from kids back home asking for support for global health programs.

CHAPTER 25

THE LOBBY MEETING

A LOBBY MEETING IS an in-person meeting with a member of Congress or an aide. The name comes from the old days when people routinely loitered in the lobby of a building to try to get face-time as members entered or exited. The term "lobbyist" now has a bad reputation as paid industry lobbyists exercise disproportionate influence over lawmakers. However, citizens who visit our own elected officials to advocate for particular causes are lobbyists, too!

Most new advocates have a very hard time imagining themselves in a lobby meeting. Although a few are eager to look a member of Congress in the eye, most are intimidated by the idea. Even so, when I take nervous first-timers along with me for a lobby meeting, they always tell me afterward that it was exciting, and they usually want to do it again!

Lobbying allows for the most personal connection and opportunities for relationship building. That's why it's the most effective form of advocacy of all. This type of action is most likely to influence a member of Congress who has not made a firm decision on an issue, so lobbying is worth all the time and energy you put into it. Senators and representatives know it's both daunting and logistically difficult for ordinary folks to meet with them in person, so they will often give more weight to our in-person requests than they give to phone calls or letters.

Because lobbying requires more time and preparation than other actions, this section will be longer than the rest. No one can predict exactly what your aide or member of Congress will say, but the more prepared you are, the better you will be able to handle unexpected situations.

Story time!

The first time I facilitated a face-to-face meeting with my congresswoman was a bit of a surprise for me. I thought my meeting would be with an aide, so I was startled when the door opened, and out came Representative Jan Schakowsky herself. I was extremely flustered and blurted out: "Hey! There you are!"

Smooth, right? I was nervous, but I was also prepared. All my practice kicked in, and the rest of the meeting went well. When the congresswoman respectfully challenged us on one of our requests, I thought my worst nightmare was happening in real life. But later, I looked back and thought, "Huh, my nightmare scenario really wasn't that bad. I did it. I can do anything!"

Before the Meeting

⤙ **Pick your issue.** Don't talk about everything that keeps you up at night. Choose one main topic and perhaps a second related issue to address if time allows.

- **Decide on your request.** Would you like them to co-sign a bill or introduce a new bill? Perhaps you need them to vote against an amendment. Be specific.
- **In a group preparation meeting, delegate roles.** Before you ever walk into the office, choose a leader to facilitate, someone to describe the issue, and someone to make your request.
- **Practice!** Whether with a group or just by yourself in front of a mirror, practice saying the words out loud so you're not tripping over any statistics or tricky terminology. Practicing for a little bit can help you be more conversational in the moment.

How to Schedule a Meeting

Scheduling a meeting with a member of Congress or an aide is a process that takes persistence. If possible, submit your meeting request a month before you want to see them, so you have plenty of time to work through these steps.

1. **Submit** a meeting request by using the office's website form. If you don't hear back in a week, move to Step 2.
2. **Call** the office for your member of Congress and determine the name and email address of the "scheduler" for the location where you want to meet (D.C. or local district office). Ask to speak to the scheduler directly with your request. If they are not available, send them an email.
3. **Follow up** every couple of days with polite emails and phone calls to the scheduler if you haven't heard back in a few days.

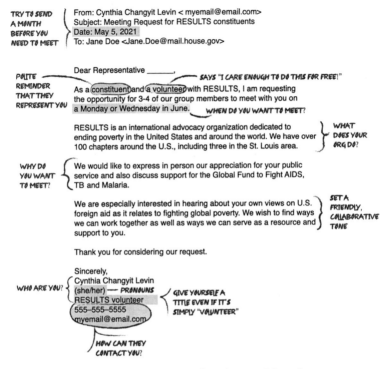

TRY TO SEND A MONTH BEFORE YOU NEED TO MEET

From: Cynthia Changyit Levin < myemail@email.com>
Subject: Meeting Request for RESULTS constituents
Date: May 5, 2021
To: Jane Doe <Jane.Doe@mail.house.gov>

Dear Representative _____,

POLITE REMINDER THAT THEY REPRESENT YOU

SAYS "I CARE ENOUGH TO DO THIS FOR FREE!"

As a constituent and a volunteer with RESULTS, I am requesting the opportunity for 3-4 of our group members to meet with you on a Monday or Wednesday in June. *WHEN DO YOU WANT TO MEET?*

WHAT DOES YOUR ORG DO?

RESULTS is an international advocacy organization dedicated to ending poverty in the United States and around the world. We have over 100 chapters around the U.S., including three in the St. Louis area.

WHY DO YOU WANT TO MEET?

We would like to express in person our appreciation for your public service and also discuss support for the Global Fund to Fight AIDS, TB and Malaria.

SET A FRIENDLY, COLLABORATIVE TONE

We are especially interested in hearing about your own views on U.S. foreign aid as it relates to fighting global poverty. We wish to find ways we can work together as well as ways we can serve as a resource and support to you.

Thank you for considering our request.

Sincerely,
Cynthia Changyit Levin
WHO ARE YOU? (she/her) — *PRONOUNS*
RESULTS volunteer
555-555-5555
myemail@email.com

GIVE YOURSELF A TITLE EVEN IF IT'S SIMPLY "VOLUNTEER"

HOW CAN THEY CONTACT YOU?

A sample meeting request email should contain all your important information.

Tips and Ideas

Tips to improve your chances of getting a meeting

- Be persistent, but not belligerent.
- Offer as much flexibility as possible for times and location.
- Accept a meeting with an aide if the congressperson is not available.
- Work with a respected nonpartisan organization.

What Should I Wear?

Most advocacy actions can be done while wearing yoga pants at home, but you'll want to look your best and convey respect in your attire for an in-person meeting or on screen. What would you wear to a worship service at a church, synagogue, or mosque if you want your appearance to convey respect to people you have never met before?

Think of a lobby meeting as a bit more casual than a job interview but more formal than a coffee date with a friend. I don't suggest wearing a suit if you don't normally wear one because you should feel as comfortable and genuine as possible.

If you are walking around Capitol Hill all day, be sure to wear comfortable shoes!

What Should I Do in the Meeting?

Every meeting is a little bit different, but I like to use this general 5-step format to keep everyone focused and on track.

1. Make Introductions

Who is in the meeting? Introduce yourself and anyone with you. Greet any aides in the room since you will probably be doing follow-up calls with them. Make sure your representative and the aides know you are a constituent and a volunteer. The fact that you live in their district means they are supposed to represent you. Your volunteerism demonstrates your personal commitment to your issue.

2. Say Thank You

Express gratitude for something the member of Congress has done on your issue recently. If they haven't done anything for you yet, thank them for making time for the meeting and for their service to our government. Many people launch right into complaints, so politeness can set you apart from the crowd.

3. Tell a Story

Use the EPIC (Engage, Problem, Inform, Call to Action) format to help you craft a short speech about your issue. Try to use a story describing something you have seen yourself, someone else's experience that you have permission to share, or an excerpt from a newspaper article. If you don't feel you have a good story, sincerely describe why the issue personally means so much to you. This is the part of the meeting where you want to emotionally connect with the aide or member of Congress.

4. Make Your Request

It is very important to make a clear request that should elicit a "yes or no" answer. The answer will likely be, "We'll look into this." Even if you get a "yes," be sure to get the name of the appropriate aide for follow-up to be sure they take your action later.

5. Ask for a Photo

A picture is not only a fun keepsake of the meeting, but it also serves as an image to post on social media along with a reminder about your request. You can still ask for a picture if you are meeting remotely on screen.

After the Meeting

Write a thank-you email to the member of Congress and/or the aide you met. If commitments were made in the meeting, repeat your understanding of them and say how much you are looking forward to seeing those things happen. Give yourself extra points if you also write another handwritten note and mail it to the office.

Call the appropriate aide about a week after the meeting. If you don't take this step, it can be like the meeting never happened at all. The aide may get busy and forget to make the phone call to put the boss's name on the bill until you call to remind them. Or the congressperson may hope you won't appear again, so any commitment made during your visit may be easily abandoned. Do not let them off that easily!

 Tips and Ideas

Tips to keep your meeting on track

Politicians like to talk. Sometimes they do it to dodge a question, but most of the time they talk because it's in their nature and they are frequently sought out for quotes. Activists get frustrated when their valuable time to present an issue is cut short by a member of Congress rambling on about a pet project. I've even had a representative pull out a laminated chart and start to lecture from it!

How can you bring the conversation back to your agenda without being rude? Try these polite pivot phrases when your congressperson is off-topic:

- "I want to be respectful of your time, so I'll get to the heart of the issue before you have to go . . ."
- "Along those same lines . . ."
- "Building on that idea . . ."
- "I see we're getting close to the end of our time together, so let me bring us to our main request . . ."

How Do I Measure Success?

You don't actually have to get a "yes" to your request to have a successful meeting. Call it a success if you manage to tell your congressperson or aides a few things about your issue that they didn't know before or if your relationship with them progresses in some way.

Volunteers often think they've done a poor job if they don't know answers to some questions that get asked. On the contrary, it's great if you prompt anyone in the room to ask tough questions. That means you got them engaged and thinking. "I don't know, but I can find out," is a perfectly acceptable answer, and it also gives you a legitimate reason to call back in a day or two. It's all part of relationship building.

If your member of Congress is strongly opposed to your position, they will probably deny your request, but your visit may plant enough thoughts to prevent them from being an active opponent. It can be a "win" just to get someone to back off and stop being a roadblock!

Anytime you listen as much as you talk, avoid name-calling and labeling, and find something that you have in common—parenting, having the same hometown, or even owning the same kind of pet—you've made a connection you can build on the next time you meet.

 Story time!

Congressman Lacy Clay engaged with our lobby team in a very congenial way, saying generally positive things about the need to address poverty in our state. There were smiles all around the table. However, just before we made the shift from talking about U.S. tax credits for low-income households to global education, I asked, "Just to be clear, before we move onto the next issue, will you co-sign the bill?"

He leaned back as if to get a clearer look at all of me and said directly, but not unkindly, "You're pushy."

Suddenly, my kids—who had been examining the stuffed toys he had given them—visibly tuned into the conversation. I could tell they were thinking, "Why is the nice man calling Mommy 'pushy'?"

I smiled more broadly as I accepted his description as a compliment. "That's probably true," I said. "It's just for clarity, you know, so my colleagues know how they should follow up with you."

Although the exchange seemed a little alarming to my kids and the newer advocates at the table, he and I both knew what had just happened. A U.S. Representative will rarely agree to sign onto an unfamiliar bill based on one office visit, but every politician would prefer that constituents feel good when they leave the office. So, they sometimes try to give an answer that feels like a "yes" even though it's a "maybe." That friendly noncommitment lets them project a supportive image without making a promise they might not want to keep.

There's nothing wrong with that. You really don't want your members of Congress to make decisions without careful consideration. But you do want to recognize when they do *not* give you a "yes." Because then you can provide more information, mobilize more advocates, or do whatever else needs to be done to seal the deal.

CHAPTER 26

THE FUNDRAISER

I INTENTIONALLY PUT THE fundraiser last on this list of actions because it is a bit problematic. Is fundraising actually the same thing as advocacy? As a former professional fundraiser for an advocacy organization, I'm here to tell you that it *can* be. Whether it is or not mostly depends upon how you design a fundraiser.

When people want to help with a cause, they often think first of fundraising. Somehow, it's what we've been trained from a young age to expect as the helpful thing to do. The American, consumer-based culture creates a general feeling that if you're not raising money for something, then you're not really helping.

A fundraiser can be an advocacy action when you engage people in conversation or action about the mission of your cause in addition to asking for money. A fundraiser can be critical outreach—especially for a new group—to tell people that your group exists and let them know how they can join you in your work.

What kinds of fundraising is *not* advocacy?

- Holding a benefit concert but never talking about your cause
- Selling cookies, bracelets, or other items without explaining why
- Offering car washes with no customer interaction

In my mind, the litmus test for advocacy is whether or not you are engaging your guests/customers/audience to be involved with your issue moving forward. Are you inviting them to know enough about your issue to become influencers themselves and rally others to the cause? What actions are you asking people to take? Asking only for money without providing education or encouraging further action is not truly advocacy.

I don't have anything against fundraisers. I'll be the first to deliver an unsolicited diatribe about how fundraising is critical for the survival of any nonprofit organization. However, I'm a volunteer and a busy mom, so I'd much rather take part in an activity that gets more bang for the buck than the actual bucks we collect. Any time you can turn a fundraiser into an opportunity for powerful advocacy, you have created a recipe for higher impact for your cause *and* a timesaver! Really—why stop at raising $300 to help build a school in Uganda when you might also influence a U.S. representative to allocate $300 million to the Global Partnership for Education?

Here are some strategies to help turn a fundraiser into an advocacy event:

- Invite a member of Congress to speak and take questions.
- Ask attendees at a fundraising event to take an action, such as sending a letter to Congress.

- Have a photographer or a reporter cover your event to publish in the media.
- Sign up attendees to take actions on your issue at a later date.

Here are three examples of fundraisers I've done with advocacy spins.

Microfinance with Girl Scouts

A Daisy troop wanted to make a microcredit loan through Kiva, an online crowdfunding site that gives small business loans to people in poverty. We read the children's book *One Hen* by Katie Smith Milway to explain microfinance in a personalized way.

The girls then raised money by asking to do special chores around the house to earn a few dollars. When they pooled their

Since not every family has spare money to donate, troop leaders must tactfully make sure everyone has a way to earn a few dollars to contribute for this activity.

money, they had enough to make a $25 loan! They chose their microcredit recipient on the Kiva website.

Then, to add that special twist of advocacy, the kids made a poster for their congresswoman about microfinance, which was delivered by one of the girls. Parents who attended the meeting wrote letters asking Congress to help support microfinance programs.

Hunger with United Methodist Church of Evanston

My church in Evanston, Illinois used to hold an "Offering of Letters" with Bread for the World each year. On a particular Sunday, congregants gathered after regular services to write to Congress about hunger. We decided to combine fundraising and letter-writing. After our pastor delivered a passionate sermon on hunger, we gathered everyone in the great hall where tables with letter-writing supplies awaited. We also set up a table full of baked goodies that could be purchased with a donation to Bread for the World.

With the letter-writing activity happening right before their eyes, people could see exactly what kind of activities their donations would support. One year, we raised enough money to pay for a volunteer to go to Washington, D.C., to the Bread for the World conference. A seamless combination of fundraising, awareness, and advocacy!

A bake sale with many different kinds of bread donated by volunteers was a perfectly themed Bread for the World event.

Global Health with Congresswoman Jan Schakowksy

My RESULTS group wanted to throw a fundraising event that would not only generate funds but also serve as an outreach and public awareness event. However, we had only a tiny group of volunteers and a small list of supporters.

So we invited our congresswoman, U.S. Representative Jan Schakowsky, to be our speaker as we knew she was very supportive of our issues. With her as a featured guest, we sold tickets to a crowd of about one hundred people who heard the congresswoman talk about the need for the U.S. to support global health programs

Congresswoman Jan Schakowsky (center) was the featured speaker for a RESULTS Chicago fundraiser.

as a means of supporting women globally. Between ticket sales and a silent auction of donated items, we raised far more than my usual bake sale events brought in. The audience even got to see citizen advocacy in action when we turned to Congresswoman Schakowsky and asked her in front of everyone to sign onto a piece of global health legislation. Happily, she agreed!

APPENDICES

GLOSSARY

Definitions of Terms Used in the Context of This Book

Act: a bill that has passed to become an official law

Activist: a person who campaigns to bring about political or social change. This could include working on legislation or public policy change.

Advocate (noun): a person who publicly supports or recommends a particular cause or policy to bring about political or social change

Advocacy: actions taken to influence government policy

Bill: a proposed piece of legislation going through the process of becoming a law

Constituent: a citizen who lives in the voting area represented by a member of Congress

House of Representatives: a governing body in the legislative branch of the U.S. government consisting of members elected from districts in a state. The number of representatives is proportional to the population of the state. There are 435 U.S. representatives.

Lobby (verb): meeting face-to-face with a member of Congress or an aide who represents them. The name comes from the days when people would loiter in the lobby of a building trying to meet with government officials.

Lobbyist: a person who meets with members of Congress or their aides to try to persuade them to take a certain position on an issue

Member of Congress: an official elected by U.S. citizens. This book generally refers to members of Congress serving in the U.S. Senate or U.S. House of Representatives. Each state also has state legislators.

Microaggression: slights, indignities, and put-downs (intentional or unintentional) that people of color, women, LGBTQ+ people and other marginalized groups experience regularly.

Mom-Advocate: a mother who expresses herself to inspire action from another person with the power to help with an issue

Representative: an elected official serving in the U.S. House of Representatives to represent people living in their district. The number of representatives in a state is determined by the population of the state.

Resolution: an official statement voted on by Congress to reflect a position held by the House of Representatives, the Senate, or both

Senate: a governing body in the legislative branch of the U.S. government. There are two senators elected from each state. There are one hundred U.S. senators.

Senator: an elected official serving in the U.S. Senate. Each senator represents the people living in their entire state.

RECOMMENDED ADVOCACY ORGANIZATIONS

OF THE GROUPS LISTED here, I have found Citizens' Climate Lobby, Friends Committee on National Legislation, and RESULTS to be especially dedicated to empowering their volunteers and dissolving powerlessness. Working with one of these three groups—even if they are not addressing your favorite cause—will prepare you with advanced advocacy skills and attitudes to have a high impact on any issue in the future.

Bread for the World

www.bread.org

Bread for the World is a collective Christian voice urging our nation's decision-makers to end hunger at home and abroad. Members mobilize churches and individuals to change policies, programs, and conditions that allow hunger and poverty to persist.

CARE

www.care-international.org

Founded in 1945, CARE is a leading humanitarian organization fighting global poverty and providing lifesaving assistance in emergencies. In one hundred countries around the world, CARE places special focus on working alongside girls and women in poverty because, equipped with the proper resources, women and girls have the power to help lift whole families and entire communities out of poverty.

Citizens' Climate Lobby (CCL)

https://citizensclimatelobby.org/

CCL is a nonprofit, nonpartisan, grassroots advocacy organization focused on national policies to address climate change. The group's consistently respectful, nonpartisan approach to climate education is designed to create a broad, sustainable foundation for climate action across all geographic regions and political inclinations.

Friends Committee on National Legislation (FCNL)

https://www.fcnl.org/

Founded by members of the Religious Society of Friends (Quakers), FCNL is a nonpartisan organization that lobbies Congress and the administration to advance peace, justice, opportunity, and environmental stewardship. It seeks a world free from war, a just and equitable society, and a sustainable planet.

Little Lobbyists

https://littlelobbyists.org/

Little Lobbyists seeks to protect and expand the rights of children who have complex medical needs and disabilities through advocacy, education, and outreach. Its vision is for all children with complex medical needs and disabilities to have access to the health care, education, and community inclusion they need to survive and thrive.

Moms Clean Air Force

https://www.momscleanairforce.org/

Moms Clean Air Force is a community of over 1,000,000 moms and dads united against air pollution—including the urgent crises of our changing climate—to protect our children's health. Through a vibrant network of state-based community organizers, members work on national and local policy issues. Their activists meet with lawmakers at every level of government and on both sides of the political aisle to build support for equitable, just, and healthy solutions to pollution.

Moms Demand Action for Gun Sense in America

https://momsdemandaction.org/

Moms Demand Action is a grassroots movement of Americans fighting for public safety measures that can protect people from gun violence. The group advocates for stronger gun laws and works to close the loopholes that jeopardize the safety of families. Members work in communities and with business leaders to encourage a culture of responsible gun ownership.

MomsRising

https://momsrising.org

MomsRising is a transformative on-the-ground and online multicultural organization of more than a million members working to increase family economic security, to end discrimination against women and mothers, and to build a nation where both businesses and families can thrive.

ONE

www.one.org

ONE is a global movement campaigning to end extreme poverty and preventable disease by 2030, so that everyone, everywhere can lead a life of dignity and opportunity. Whether lobbying political leaders in world capitals or running cutting-edge grassroots campaigns, ONE pressures governments to do more to fight extreme poverty and preventable disease, particularly in Africa, and empowers citizens to hold their governments accountable.

RESULTS

www.results.org

RESULTS is an international movement of passionate, committed everyday people using their voices to influence political decisions that will bring an end to poverty. Volunteers receive training, support, and inspiration to become skilled advocates. In time, volunteers learn to effectively advise policymakers, guiding them towards decisions that improve access to education, health, and economic opportunity.

Shot@Life

https://shotatlife.org/

Shot@Life is a campaign of the United Nations Foundation that champions global childhood immunization. The group rallies members of the public and Congress, businesses, and civil society partners to support the cause and invest in the immunization programs of UNICEF, the World Health Organization, and Gavi, the Vaccine Alliance. It strives to decrease vaccine-preventable childhood deaths and give all children a shot at a healthy life no matter where they live.

NOTES AND SOURCES

Chapter 1
How I Became the "Anti-Poverty Mom"

1. World Health Organization report, "World Health Statistics 2020: Monitoring Health for the Sustainable Development Goals," https://www.who.int/publications/i/item/9789240005105
2. "Chicago's Promise to Kenya," WBEZ 91.5 Chicago, updated February 13, 2007, https://www.wbez.org/stories/chicagos-promise-to-kenya/82fa3458-33f7-4fe3-bbe1-884c4f2e5cb9
3. A "trim tab" is a nautical term referring to a small rudder that makes adjustments to assist a bigger rudder in the steering of a large ship. Here, "trimtabbing" is a metaphor for engaged citizens influencing members of Congress to assist in the steering of the government, sometimes referred to as the "ship of state."
4. "What Have the Millennium Achievement Goals Achieved," The Guardian, July 6, 2015, http://www.theguardian.com/global-development/datablog/2015/jul/06/what-millennium-development-goals-achieved-mdgs

Chapter 2
What Does a Mom-Advocate Do?

5. Watty Piper, *The Little Engine That Could* (New York: Platt and Munk 1930).

Chapter 3
Why Should Moms Be Advocates?

6. R. Feldman, A. Weller, O. Zagoory-Sharon, & A. Levine, "Evidence for a Neuroendocrinological Foundation of Human Affiliation: Plasma Oxytocin Levels Across Pregnancy and the Postpartum Period Predict Mother-Infant Bonding," Psychological Science (November 2007).

7. Fred Rogers testimony, U.S. Senate Subcommittee on Communications, May 1, 1969, https://www.youtube.com/watch?v=fKy7ljRr0AA

Chapter 4
Profile: Columba Sainz, Interlocking Issues

8. American Lung Association, "Most Polluted Cities," https://www.stateoftheair.org/

Chapter 5
What Difference Can One Mom Make?

9. UNICEF report, "Levels & Trends in Child Mortality, Report 2020, Estimates developed by the UN Inter-agency Group for Child Mortality Estimation," https://www.unicef.org/media/79371/file/UN-IGME-child-mortality-report-2020.pdf

Chapter 7
Can Advocacy Make Your Life Better?

10. "With Kids in the House, Mothers Are Less Satisfied," ScienceNorway.no, February 3, 2012, https://sciencenorway.no/forskningno-norway-pregnancy/with-kids-in-the-house-mothers-are-less-satisfied/1450402

11. P. L. Dalgas-Pelish, "The Impact of the First Child on Marital Happiness," Journal of Advanced Nursing 18, no. 3 (March 1993): 437–41; https://onlinelibrary.wiley.com/doi/abs/10.1046/j.1365-2648.1993.18030437.x

Chapter 11
Profile: Teresa Rugg, Advocating
Your Own Way

12. USAID report, "Two Decades of Progress: USAID'S Child Survival and Maternal Health Program," June 2009, https://reliefweb.int/sites/reliefweb.int/files/resources/9DA4BA546D46FA41492575D80006C4DF-USAID_Jun2009.pdf

13. UNICEF report, "The State of the World's Children 1987," Author: James P. Grant, https://www.unicef.org/media/90251/file/SOWC-1987.pdf

14. UNICEF report, "Levels & Trends in Child Mortality, Report 2020, Estimates developed by the UN Inter-agency Group for Child Mortality Estimation," https://www.unicef.org/media/79371/file/UN-IGME-child-mortality-report-2020.pdf; and World Health Organization, "COVID-19 Could Reverse Decades of Progress Toward Eliminating Preventable Child Deaths, Agencies Warn," Sept. 9, 2020, https://www.who.int/news/item/09-09-2020-covid-19-could-reverse-decades-of-progress-toward-eliminating-preventable-child-deaths-agencies-warn

Chapter 14
Step Out of Your Comfort Zone

15. L. Brenson, "Racial Diversity Among Top Staff in Senate Personal Offices," Joint Center for Political and Economic Studies, August 2020, https://jointcenter.org/racial-diversity-among-top-staff-in-senate-personal-offices/

Part III
Advocacy Made Easy

16. Bradford Fitch, Kathy Goldschmidt, & Nicole Folk Cooper, "Citizen-Centric Advocacy: The Untapped Power of Constituent Engagement," Congressional Management Foundation, 2017, http://www.congressfoundation.org/storage/documents/CMF_Pubs/cmf-citizen-centric-advocacy.pdf

WHERE DO I START?
(THE SHORT ANSWER)

WELCOME TO THE BACK of the book! Perhaps you finished the whole thing or maybe you took my advice in the introduction and skipped around until you got here. Or maybe you just like to start with the last page of the book.

Regardless of how you arrived, if you're impatient to start being a world changer, I strongly encourage you to connect with a reputable, nonpartisan advocacy organization. Taking action is so much easier when you personally connect with others for inspiration and education. Engaging regularly with others also helps you hold each other accountable to make sure you stay in action.

Look for organizations that are dedicated to empowering volunteers. These groups are as passionate about helping you develop your own individual voice as they are about advancing their causes. In the appendices, you'll find a list called "Recommended Advocacy Organizations" and a couple of my recommendations for groups placing volunteer empowerment at the heart of their structure and core values. These groups can nourish your advocacy skills and attitudes so that you can have a high impact on any issue and with any organization in the future.

Finally, let me leave you with a bit of advice from Becky Morgan, mom of two and Missouri Chapter Leader at Moms Demand Action for Gun Sense in America:

> Do what is comfortable for you. Just find something that works for you. If it's tweeting, if it's a phone call, start there. Become comfortable with that and work your way up to talking to a lawmaker face-to-face when you're ready. Jump in, find what you are comfortable with, and don't let anyone take your voice away.